My Redemption from Pluto:

Lessons Learned from Life's Relationships

By Larry V. Dykstra

Inspired Forever Books
Dallas, Texas

AUCTOREM
HOUSE

Auctorem House
276 5th Ave, Ste 704-2591
New York, NY 10001
www.auctoremhouse.com
Phone: 1 888-332-7718

Published by Auctorem House: 03/18/2026

ISBN: 978-1-968059-36-1(sc)
ISBN: 978-1-968059-37-8(e)

Library of Congress Control Number: 2026902052

To all lifetime learners, regardless of the age indicated by their birth certificates.

You're going to feel like hell if you wake up someday and you never wrote the stuff that is tugging on the sleeves of your heart: your stories, memories, visions and songs—your truth, your version of things—in your own voice. That's really all you have to offer us; and that's also why you were born.

—Anne Lamott
"12 Things I Know for Sure," TED2017

Table of Contents

Introduction

My memory tilts toward stories, not numbers or names. But only certain ones endure. I think the stories that stick represent moments when I was exposed to some new and deeper level of understanding of myself, others, the world around me, and the transcendent. Those stories of significance remain vivid to me.

It was that kind of moment that initiated this work. My friend and former colleague from my time working at Pizza Hut, Robin, was the victim of a cancer she fought with perseverance and grace. Her positive spirit should have made her a winner in this battle. Sadly, it didn't.

I was honored to play guitar and sing for her four times in the hospital and at her home the evening before she passed away. During one hospital visit, she requested I play the last song on Warren Zevon's final album, a poignant farewell titled "Keep Me in Your Heart," which had been released two months before his death from cancer. When a doctor entered Robin's room on an official visit, I suggested it was time for me to leave and started packing my guitar in its case.

"No, Larry," said Robin. "Play that song." And so I did. Robin turned to her doctor after I finished and said, "He is going to sing that song at my memorial service."

A couple of months later, I sang it again, accompanied by her husband, who blew past his grief into a harmonica.

Following the service, friends and colleagues convened in a nearby watering hole to toast her memory. There were at least one hundred of us present that afternoon, a testament to the power and reach of Robin's vibrant character. After an hour of visiting, I was preparing to leave the scene when I spotted Mary, a long-term colleague, and decided to offer her a quick hello and goodbye.

Mary was chatting with Carl, an executive who had joined Pizza Hut just before I'd left the organization after fourteen years. Carl and I had been two marketing professionals passing on opposite panels of the corporate revolving door. We were friendly but not friends—collegial but not colleagues. We had shared time in staff meetings but had never worked together on the kind of initiative where the stakes were high, and we were forced to struggle through challenges that forge and temper strong relationships.

Around the time Carl started, I had agreed to stay on for my final year with an assignment to build organizational know-how, which primarily meant training the growing number of new team members in our company's consumer-driven insight and innovation processes. I had liked the idea of teaching, a way to leverage my experience and give something back as my career was winding down. I had expected newer members of the marketing department would come knocking on my door, seeking out my wisdom. When they did not, I had sunk into a funk about my own self-worth.

Around this same time, the International Astronomic Association had voted that Pluto no longer met the definition of a planet. Pluto's problem was that it was out of sync with its neighbors, just like my orbit with my colleagues. A new verb had been introduced into the English language: *plutoed*, meaning "to demote or devalue someone or something." The word had become so popular that the American Dialect Society had declared *plutoed* its 2006 word of the year. *Plutoed* described how I had felt.

After I had briefly talked with Mary, Carl leaned in and said, "Larry, that presentation you made to the marketing department before you left was great. The lessons you shared were so valuable that I have used them as a coaching tool with my direct reports."

I felt simultaneously proud and hurt. Others had complimented me on what I had presented a few years earlier, so I was confident the insights I shared that day were of value. But Carl's comment opened the gate for two contradictory thoughts to jockey for the lead position of my consciousness. The first—"You gave me credit, right?"—I wisely kept to myself. The second, more constructive contestant lingered for weeks: "Maybe I should look it over to see what I said." The seeds of this book were sowed.

The presentation in question had been made during the first week in February 2009, the day before I walked out of my corporate office for the last time to wander into early retirement. It would be my last of hundreds of business presentations, one that I had initiated as a parting gift to my audience of forty-five colleagues in the marketing department. Some present, such as Robin, I had worked with for all of fourteen years. Most, like Carl, were newer to the organization. My goal had been to share one "truth" for each year of my career. The title, quite simply, was "25 Things I Learned in 25 Years in Business."

When I reviewed the presentation, most of the lessons still resonated with me. I saw that most reflected human truths, not business truths. While I may have experienced many of them in the corporate context, they applied more broadly. Plus, a lot had happened in my life in the decade since it had been written, so the list had grown beyond the original twenty-five.[1]

Four questions guided my way to a revised list of lessons:

- What was the inciting incident that triggered each lesson?

- What stood out in my memory of how I experienced each one?

- What did I learn as a result?

- How is this experience applicable to others?

As I reflected on each learning, I realized each deserved a stage, set, and storyline all its own that revealed its truth.

In his recent best-selling book *From Strength to Strength: Finding Success, Happiness, and Deep Purpose in the Second Half of Life*, Arthur C. Brooks explained that people tend to be in denial about age-related performance decline, which he asserted happens earlier than we might think (between the ages of thirty-five and fifty).[2] He described the differences between *fluid intelligence* (the ability to reason and solve abstract problems, which peaks when we are young) and *crystallized intelligence* (the ability to apply our knowledge, which increases with age). Brooks suggested that rather than resist the inevitable decline in *fluid intelligence* as we mature, we should leverage our growing *crystallized intelligence* by sharing our wisdom with others.

I wish I had the benefit of Mr. Brooks's advice when I was finding it difficult to accept the changing trajectory of my career path. Instead of viewing my final corporate assignment to "build know-how" as a job title devoid of serious responsibilities, I should have embraced it as a meaningful way to add value by using my experience to help others. Today, I see it as a missed opportunity because I believed a false narrative that I had little left to offer. In short, I fell into the bad company of Pluto.

Sins of omission take longer to recognize and accept. With the benefit of hindsight, I wonder why I failed to reach out to my colleagues and ask about the challenges they faced and if I could lend a helping hand, whether that be insight into past marketing successes and failures or how to navigate the wide range of decision-making tendencies of key players in the organization, which I knew very well. This book is my attempt at redemption, to make up for my failure to seize the opportunity that once lay right in front of me by sharing lessons I learned from four types of relationships we develop in life.

These stories go to the core of who I am: an imperfect but loved child of God. I offer them as a pathway into your personal learning. Please read them with an open heart and mind. Try to place yourself in the narrative. Consider what you are thinking and feeling while you engage with these words. And, if you are so inclined, make these lessons your own.

Better yet, follow Anne Lamott's advice from the epigraph, and take the time to write your own truth in your own voice.

Peace.

---

[1] The twenty-five learnings from the original list can be found in the appendix.
[2] Arthur C. Brooks, *From Strength to Strength: Finding Success, Happiness, and Deep Purpose in the Second Half of Life* (Brentford: Portfolio, 2022).

Author's Note

There are countless ways to organize a book comprised of multiple, unrelated stories. My initial inclination was to offer these stories in a shapeless form like the original "25 Things" presentation. Providing no logical flow or structure would allow readers to engage with the stories in the manner with which life engages us—unfolding with no particular or discernable pattern or trajectory. I suspect readers expect more than that from a writer, so I demanded it of myself.

One logical approach would have been to arrange these personal stories around the timeline of my life. I abandoned this idea for two reasons: (1) I have little interest in producing a personal memoir, and (2) my life journey has taken so many unexpected twists and turns that this approach may confuse more than illuminate. I will, however, include information about the place and time of each story to help provide readers with limited yet relevant context.

As I considered other organizing options, I realized individual chapters fell into one of four distinct categories or themes: (1) my understanding of myself, (2) my relationships with others, (3) my appreciation of the world around me, and (4) my awareness and connection with the transcendent power of God. This framework mirrors the concept of *relational consciousness* developed by David Hay and Rebecca Nye through their research on spirituality in children.[1] Based on interviews with children aged ten and under, Hay and Nye concluded that while young children may not have developed the formal religious language to express their inner spiritual nature, they possessed an intuitive awareness of four different relationships that shaped their understanding of who they were as individuals. Hay and Nye called these Child-Self Consciousness, Child-People Consciousness, Child-World Consciousness, and Child-God Consciousness.

I have chosen different language for these relationships, depicted in the following

illustration.

(FIGURE A HERE)

While some of these stories may touch on more than one of these dimensions, I have

assigned them to sections based on what I sensed was the primary truth revealed through these

experiences and why they held special meaning to me. You may feel some stories better fit a

different category. I accept that as a positive sign of your engagement in the material, for which I

say "Thank you."

---

[1] David Hay and Rebecca Nye, *The Spirit of the Child*, rev. ed. (London: Jessica Kingsley Publishers, 2006).

Part I: Self

Like a lot of people I know, I spend most of each day in my own company, absorbed in personal movements and thoughts. I used to think being the center of my own attention would allow me to know myself pretty well, or at least better than anyone else knows me. I see now that understanding one's "self" is a journey that requires distance, time, and an occasional external nudge.

I am now in my seventies, an age that offers a vantage point where I can observe my past from a safe distance. One of the more interesting discoveries I made was that I did not become who I am today on my own. My personal growth journey was prompted by an intentional comment, something I observed in others, or incidents that forced me to recognize something in myself that needed to be addressed. Regardless of source, each, in its own way, challenged me to reconsider assumptions about who I truly am.

So I begin with stories that share what I have done and seen and felt and learned on my path toward coming into relationship with my own identity. They are stories that define the "self" I am today and prime me for the better one I hope to become tomorrow.

Chapter One

A New Spin on the Curveball

Ah, the curveball! In baseball, regardless of playing position, mastery of the breaking ball guards the gateway dividing success from failure. For pitchers, it is impossible to make the big leagues if they are unable to throw a good one, and batters won't stay there if they can't hit one.

I developed the ability to throw an effective curve at a young age. My father, who gifted me with his willingness to spend countless hours catching my practice pitches in the yard behind our farmhouse, testified he did not teach me. I doubt my training came from my junior league coaches, who volunteered their time and attention, not their technical expertise, to support local youth. Since I grew up in the 1960s, when knowledge wasn't a Google search away, how or where I learned to throw a curveball remains a mystery.

That was how most batters I faced around the age of thirteen viewed my breaking ball—a mystery. In baseball lingo, mine could be called a *jug-handle curve*, descriptive of its broad sweeping arc that mimicked the handle of a water pitcher. Partnered with a solid fastball, my curve bewildered most young players, resulting in a competitive advantage that made me, on my best days, unstoppable.

My poor junior league catcher also found it unstoppable. Even when he knew the pitch was coming, Bobby would grasp for air as the ball flew past his waving mitt. Since there was no base stealing in our games, the only penalty was the delay following each pitch while he retrieved the ball lying on the ground near the backstop a few feet behind home plate.

By the time I was a junior in high school, I was able to control the pitch's trajectory with great accuracy. When baseball season arrived in the Midwest, which was long before weather suitable for the sport did, I recall inexperienced freshmen players stepping up to a taped shape of home plate on the gym floor. After a couple of fastballs straight down the middle to establish expectations, I would unleash my curve. Having thrown it for years and being confident with the magnitude of its break, I would aim the pitch at the head of a right-handed hitter, knowing it would move from the two o'clock position and toward eight o'clock. I can still see the looks on their faces, how their eyes would grow open and large as the ball swooped in like a fierce raptor attacking from out of nowhere. Many would seek safety by diving out of the batter's box as the pitch slid downward and into the center of the strike zone. From that moment on, it didn't matter what pitch I threw to these hitting novices. I owned them.

For many years, I was proud of how the movement of my curveball confounded most hitters I faced. But then, at the occasion of my brother-in-law's memorial service, a former high school teammate whom I hadn't seen in over forty years made a comment that shed new light on both the pitch and my usage of it.

"You used to scare the daylights out of me," said Adam.

"What do you mean?" I asked.

"Your curveball . . . I had never seen anything like it. I remember having to hit against you in practice . . . and it scared me to death!"

My mind raced back to those indoor practice sessions. Before my former teammate's comment, I had never considered how batting practice could devolve into an act of bullying. I had chosen to believe I was demonstrating my athletic prowess. But Adam's comment exposed my curveball for how others saw it—a weapon of terror I'd used to frighten members of my own team. (Since it is never too late to apologize, if any of you are reading this fifty years later, I am truly sorry.)

I am guessing Adam did not remember the regional playoff game during my junior year. Since our regular season schedule paired us against other small high schools with players unfamiliar with the pitch, my curveball was a dominant factor in most games. In the regional playoffs, we were pitted against one of the bigger schools from Kankakee, Illinois, the largest city in the county. Early in that game, I got ahead on the count against their right-handed cleanup hitter by throwing two well-placed fastballs.

"It is time for the curve," I thought to myself. "He is set up for it. He'll be looking for another fastball."

I threw the next pitch with complete confidence. The replay booth of my memory shifts to slow motion as the ball leaves my hand. The pitch starts high and inside, right where I aimed it—at the batter's helmet. I remember the look on his face, how his eyes grew open and large. But these were focused eyes, not fearful ones. The batter had locked in on my pitch's predictable sweeping arc. As it reached the plate, he connected (here's where the replay returns to full speed), and the ball was catapulted fast and far over the left field fence.

Many of his teammates also feasted on my curveball that day. From the pitcher's mound, I watched a parade of runners round the bases on their way to our lopsided defeat. What had stymied novice hitters was my flawed gift to these skilled ones. My curveball was no longer a mystery or a competitive advantage; it had become a liability.

I learned a lesson that day about how personal strengths, particularly towering ones, can grow to be weaknesses in disguise. It is a principle that applies beyond the baseball diamond to include personal traits (high standards taken too far become perfectionism) as well as organizational characteristics (impressive size and scale lead to an inability to adapt to a changing environment). Since what contributes to success is likely to change with time, it is critical to *keep learning, adjusting, and growing.*

During the next season as a high school senior, I experimented with refinements to my signature pitch, but nothing felt as natural as the version I had thrown for years. I was unable to find a new spin on my curveball. Maybe I lacked the commitment or discipline required to evolve and stay on top of my game. Fortunately, in time I would discover role models from vastly different fields who would demonstrate what it takes to stay ahead of the curve.

Chapter Two

A Lesson in More than Geography

He paced across the front of the stuffy classroom with a globe cradled under his left arm. Beads of sweat dampened the graying hair near his temples while his blue eyes sparkled behind wire-rimmed glasses. Pausing, the professor turned and pointed at the large map of the world hanging on the wall and declared a concept as if it were a major scientific discovery reported in today's headlines: "The vorld is not flat; the vorld is round!" Then, in case we hadn't heard it correctly, he repeated the statement, the timbre of his Dutch brogue stronger this time: *"The vorld is not flat! The vorld is round!"*

I wrote down his every word in my three-ring notebook. Never had knowledge been imparted to me with such passion. Dr. Hamming spoke with such clarity and conviction that day I suspect even the staunchest member of the Flat Earth Society would have been converted.

I was a senior at Augustana College in Illinois at the time and had fulfilled nearly all course requirements for my political science major. That fall semester offered me the luxury of enrolling in lower-level introductory courses in subjects such as geography, philosophy, and American short stories. It turned out to be my most authentic college educational experience because I approached each class with the mature goal of learning something new.

Dr. Hamming's Geography of Transportation was one of those elective classes, covering topics such as the logic behind the numbering of our interstate highway system, the location of major railroad lines, and navigational paths such as the "great circle route." The latter refers to the path transatlantic flights follow over polar lands such as Iceland and Nova Scotia on trips between North America and Europe. To demonstrate the shortest distance between North

America and Europe, Dr. Hamming stretched a piece of string over the surface of his globe to show how much shorter that route was compared to following a latitude across the Atlantic. Knowing that the world is round allows international air carriers to save significant time and fuel.

Dr. Hamming was making a deeper technical point that day. By juxtaposing the image of the spherical globe with the flatness of the wall map, Dr. Hamming demonstrated how the visual version of the world we see printed in atlases (called the Mercator projection after sixteenth-century Flemish geographer and cartographer Gerardus Mercator) exaggerates the size of the landmasses located closer to either pole. Greenland and Antarctica may be huge, but the flat map portrays them as much larger than they actually are compared to landmasses closer to the equator. Because the world is indeed round, our most accurate understanding of the relative size of countries and continents comes by studying a spherical globe, not a two-dimensional map.

We all know by fourth grade that the world is round, so Dr. Hamming was not offering any new wisdom. It was the utter zeal with which he shared this common knowledge that impressed me in that moment and has stuck with me ever since. I recall wondering, "How can he be so excited about something we already understand and that he has been teaching for dozens of years?"

Today, I see there was much more being shared with me that day than a simple lesson in geography from a paid academic. Dr. Hamming offered testimony to how passion for his work inspired his long career and, by extension, every student fortunate enough to beat the odds and enroll in his popular classes. It was impossible to miss how much Dr. Hamming loved what he did for a living, his genuine care and concern for his students, the tireless enthusiasm for the concepts from his field of study, and the unbridled energy with which he communicated them.

Before I heard Dr. Hamming utter those nine words, I had known that the world was round; I just had never *felt* it. His passion for his work produced that effect on me.

I shared these thoughts with Bruce Hamming, my former college roommate, teammate, and friend, as well as the son of Professor Hamming. In response, he wrote:

Your comment about how he had taught the same course for many years and still had the passion reminds me of one event. Once, my dad was preparing a lecture for the next day and I asked him why he was rewriting a lecture for a class he had taught so many times before. It is not like geography was rapidly changing like history or physics. His reply was, "It is a new year with new students, and I need to keep it fresh. I might say things differently in a better way for them to understand." I remember being impressed by that because it was obvious that some other teachers were just regurgitating the same material they had used for their entire teaching career. Like you say, the difference was passion.

The concept of *flow* comes to mind when I think of Dr. Hamming's approach to his lectures at that small liberal arts college. Named by positive psychologist Mihály Csíkszentmihályi, *flow* is the mental state where a person becomes so absorbed in what they are doing that they lose the sense of space, time, and self-consciousness. Their activity is so intrinsically rewarding that other needs become negligible or disappear from conscious thinking. You have most likely heard this phenomenon described in sports as an athlete being "in the zone," where actions seem natural and effortless. Dr. Hamming taught "in the zone."

Imagine what it would be like if our jobs produced *flow* experiences. Since succeeding in a career requires one to remain engaged in its substance over the long haul, possessing a genuine passion for our work might provide the energy we need to master our expertise and produce greater results. Finding even one element of our work that engages the mind and excites the soul might do the trick. Perhaps your sense of flow appears through the camaraderie of working with a team, seeing your ideas become reality, or just being a part of a meaningful mission. Regardless, since a full-time job requires 40 percent of one's waking hours (a conservative estimate), why would we strive for anything less?

So *pursue your passion*, whatever that may be. If you can't find a path to passion through career or job, try to do that in the remaining 60 percent of the time you are awake. In my case, my passion for music was the starting point on a journey into finding meaningful volunteer service. Upon my retirement, I started with something I truly enjoyed doing (playing guitar and singing with others), opened myself to suggestions regarding places where my skills and passion might be useful (the day care center at work), paid close attention to how others responded to it and how this experience felt for me (rewarding), and extended that activity into new contexts (hospitals, nursing homes). In time, my journey took me to a sweet spot where my personal passion intersected with a real human need (playing music to severely ill children and their caregivers in hospitals). There, I would experience *flow* because my service demanded I be fully present for others. There, I found my music mattered, and by extension, so did I.

When I think back to that lecture in the fall of my senior year, I can see and hear Dr. Hamming's lecture as if it were yesterday. That's how great lessons work. That's how great teachers teach. That is how passion cuts through the quiet drudgery of life, grabs our attention, and keeps us going over the long haul. Beyond setting the record straight regarding the true shape and dimension of our earth, Dr. Hamming demonstrated something more important: how tapping into one's passion can lead to a life that is rich and full, not flat.

Chapter Three

A Prescription for Happiness

I chuckled out loud when I read the bumper sticker on the car stopped in front of me. That doesn't happen very often—the audible laughter, that is. I could blame it on my Midwestern roots, a place where both joy and anger tend to be suppressed, lest you call too much attention to yourself. Or maybe it's inherent in my nature. Regardless, today I am able to laugh out loud when the moment is right, like when a four-word phrase captures wisdom in such a succinct way: "Bark Less, Wag More."

The quote reminded me of Patch Adams, made famous by Robin Williams's portrayal in his biographical movie. Adams challenged medical practices he believed dehumanized patients by dealing with them as subjects who required treatment rather than real people who needed to be engaged in their own healing. The medical establishment felt threatened by his attempts to bring humor into their serious domain, with one supervisor criticizing Adams for "excessive happiness" on his performance evaluation. Aided by Dr. Adams's pioneering efforts, hospitals today welcome clowns, therapy dogs, and musicians like me because they understand the power a little good cheer can bring to a place that can administer heavy doses of fear.

No one ever accused me of "excessive happiness" at work or home. The phrase "excessive stoicism" might better describe my serious approach to work and life. I view it as an ethic rooted in my agrarian upbringing. I was taught the basic tenet of employment was that the wages of work demanded keeping one's head down and nose to the proverbial grindstone.

It was not like I wasn't aware of the serious affect I wore like a cheap suit in the workplace. I was fortunate to have a colleague willing to point out the countless ways I could be more effective. That person was Chris, my administrative assistant, who had a knack for spotting and naming the truth circling around any situation. She was direct when offering her advice, like the way she shared two simple words with me on multiple occasions. "Lighten up," she would say. Despite her regular reminders, I remained locked in a pattern of behavior that was anchored in the opposite end of the workplace happiness continuum from Patch Adams. I was able to have fun at times, but those moments were the exceptions during my professional career.

An unmistakable lesson on the power of "lightening up" arrived in a context far away from my work. My teenage son, Evan, and I had signed up to be cast members in our church's production of *Amahl and the Night Visitors*. This one-act opera written by Gian Carlo Menotti follows the wise men as they journey to bring gifts to the Christ child. During their trip, they arrive at the home of a young boy named Amahl and his mother and ask for a place to rest for the evening. The plot thickens as the poor family is tempted by the riches these magi are carrying to the newborn king.

Evan and I assumed we would be singers in the thirty-member cast, but Ken, the director of music at our church, had grander plans. Ken possessed an uncanny ability to maneuver me (and others) into accepting assignments without revealing all that might be required. Such was the case here. Despite our lack of talent and experience, a gentleman named Kevin, Evan, and I were cast as dancers who would perform for the magi at the midpoint of the play. Our part consisted of a series of dance steps with three young women, which required additional rehearsals. At times, I questioned why we needed to commit to so much work for just two performances of a scene only four minutes long.

To help us learn our moves, a professional choreographer was assigned the challenge of transforming us into three graceful couples. Our awkwardness tested her patience at first, but with time and effort, we improved. However, my worries about how family and friends attending the play would assess our footwork remained.

When we concluded the final rehearsal, our choreographer huddled her six students together to offer parting words of encouragement and advice. "You've each practiced hard, and you're ready," she said. "There is only one thing you need remember when you are onstage the next two nights."

I leaned in, anticipating a last tidbit of technical direction that would ensure flawless execution of our dance routine.

"All you have to do is smile."

"Huh?" I protested to myself. "That's it?"

"If *you* look like you are having fun," she continued, "the audience will notice and enjoy your performance. So just smile."

I don't remember if I smiled much during our performances, but I recall how audiences on both nights applauded our dance routine. We even overcame one mishap when Evan and Kevin got their feet tangled and the latter crashed to the floor. Those attending that performance thought it was a planned pratfall due to Kevin's catlike ability to scramble back to his feet and continue dancing, smiling all the way through the fall and recovery.

In the months and years ahead, I began to apply this "just smile" advice to other aspects of my life. I paid closer attention to the faces of performers at concerts or speaking events, and I noticed the performances I appreciated most were when those onstage seemed to be enjoying themselves. As I prepared to sing with my bandmates or in choral groups, I would draw little smiley faces on the sheet music as a visual reminder to project a sense of joy. "I love playing music," I thought, "so why not show it?" The approach worked wonders, as I felt a closer connection to both my bandmates and the audience.

I began to "just smile" in other aspects of my daily life, such as during trips to the grocery store or visits to the gym. I discovered that when I behaved like I was enjoying what I was doing, I felt happier inside. This reversed my assumption about how change occurs: that new beliefs precede new behaviors. I found that the opposite order works as well—perhaps better. As I consciously forced myself to smile more, my orientation toward life improved. My way of behaving changed my way of feeling, and because smiling made me feel good inside, I saw that others responded in kind.

Smiling is contagious and nearly impossible to resist. When we smile at someone else, chances are they will smile back. This is due to the fact that humans have the innate ability to mimic the emotions of others. When we see emotions expressed on the faces of others (positive or negative), a similar emotional state is created in our brains.

The benefits that come from smiling may extend beyond the immediate moment. In a thirty-year study, UC Berkeley researchers found that individuals with bigger and broader smiles in their yearbook pictures had longer and more fulfilling marriages and scored higher on tests of well-being. Another study from Wayne State University revealed that professional baseball players who smiled for their 1952 trading card photos lived an average of seven years longer than those who did not.[1]

Years later, I find our choreographer's final advice to "just smile" to be one of the most profound insights ever shared with me. It took me time to apply and discover its power, but today I smile more than I did during my work days. While that may be partly due to the fact that I am no longer in a stressful office setting every day, I believe most of the credit comes from the fact that I changed my way of acting—and a new way of feeling followed. Telling myself that I should "lighten up" couldn't move me to change, but smiling more did.

Don't take my word for it. The next time you are wandering around a public place or passing through a TSA checkpoint on your way to a flight, identify someone who doesn't seem to be having a very good day. Give them a smile. Chances are they will smile back, and you will both feel better.

So *bark less and wag more.* It is a prescription for happiness I suspect Dr. Patch Adams would write for us all.

---

[1] Eric Savitz, "The Untapped Power of Smiling" *Forbes*, March 22, 2011, CIO Next,
https://www.forbes.com/sites/ericsavitz/2011/03/22/the-untapped-power-of-smiling/#b4d5e1d7a67b.

Chapter Four

A Terrible Thing to Waste

We had conquered numerous difficult ascents, but this climb felt harder. The midday sun beat down as we made our way up the steep road just outside the town of Castrojeriz, Spain. After multiple pauses to recapture our motivation and gaze back at the valley floor behind us, we reached the summit named Alto de Mostelares and caught our first panoramic view of what lay ahead—the *meseta*. Golden wheat fields glimmered as far as the eye could see, dotted here and there by small buildings scattered across the plain. A sun-drenched path snaked onward until it disappeared into the western horizon. "And we have to walk through all of that!" I complained to myself.

The year was 2012, and this was the eleventh of my twenty-nine consecutive days on the Camino de Santiago, a pilgrimage route that crosses northern Spain. Individuals have been walking the route for over one thousand years from points scattered throughout Europe. Legend has it that the remains of Jesus's apostle Saint James the Elder lie entombed in the Cathedral of Santiago. Since the Middle Ages, Christians have trekked to this cathedral, hoping to be healed of their ailments. Today, most pilgrims walk for recreational or spiritual reasons.

My wife, Sandy, and I took our first steps as pilgrims from Pamplona, Spain, near the French border. To be an official pilgrim, or *peregrino*, one must acquire something akin to a passport called the *credencial del peregrino*. This document is stamped at locations along the route to allow admission to *albergues*, facilities like a youth hostel or dormitory with bunk beds, communal showers, and toilet facilities for the price of five to ten euros a night. We experienced rooms with as few as eight pilgrims and others housing more than one hundred. It was a communal form of living where enthusiastic snoring occurred every night, making earplugs a necessity.

The Camino, also called the Way of Saint James, is comprised of three distinct sections. Heading west from the French border, the first section passes through the Rioja region, where walkers are treated to a gently rolling countryside of farms and vineyards. The final section traverses the region called Galicia, where the cooler and damper climate supports a verdant green landscape rich in vegetation. In between awaits the meseta.

Life on the Camino is simple, social, and solitary. For the meseta, more ominous words come to mind. I had read about this middle section in guidebooks, which described it as "boring, repetitive, and bleak" or "lifeless and desolate." Many pilgrims avoid this segment by taking a two-hundred-kilometer bus ride from Burgos to Leon, the two major Spanish cities that bookend the section. We chose to walk the meseta because we thought we understood the challenge it posed. We were wrong.

Walking the meseta was a wilderness experience that challenged both my body and spirit. While the flat terrain made each step easy, the barren landscape stripped away any feeling of progress. Midday temperatures over 40 degrees Celsius (104 Fahrenheit) sapped our strength with each step.

It was on this barren stretch of the Camino where my energy faded. The sun felt hotter than normal as it beat down through a cloudless sky. There was nothing in sight for miles, only a narrow road that appeared to wind on for an eternity. My drinking water had become lukewarm. I had stopped talking to Sandy miles before. When I spotted a lone tree along the side of the road, I walked toward its shade, threw down my walking stick, muttered something like "This is stupid," and told Sandy to continue without me. She was happy to oblige.

I sat down under the tree, partly to rest but more to bask in my regret for the temper tantrum. I scolded myself for the meltdown and took a big gulp of tepid water to chase down the personal pride I needed to swallow.

I recalled the book buried deep inside my backpack—*Man's Search for Meaning*, written by Viktor Frankl following his three-year internment in a Nazi concentration camp during World War II.[1] A prominent Jewish psychiatrist before the war, Frankl observed his fellow inmates and noted that those most likely to survive the ordeal were able to find some sustaining purpose in life. Frankl concluded that, even in the face of the most horrible conditions and treatment, as humans we still retain the freedom to choose how we react to whatever challenge we may be facing.

Underneath the shade of that tree, Frankl's core message became real for me. My tantrum had done nothing to remove the challenges still before me. To reach my destination, I would need to convert my frustration into a positive spirit.

Even though my little hissy fit incident happened thousands of miles from my work and home, I recalled times when I could have benefited from Dr. Frankl's wisdom. It would have come in handy when I was assigned a new boss or work assignment not to my liking, or on those occasions when I was required to attend a mandatory team-building activity that distracted from more pressing needs. Because I failed to embrace these situations in a positive way, my attitude hindered me from being my best and making the most of the situation.

Our worst moments may not always be as obvious and immediate as my meseta meltdown was for me. It is easy to get caught up in the urgent demands of the moment and fail to recognize how our mindset can impact both the experience and outcome. Be prepared to use your mindset to your advantage, because a situation that displays the signs of a challenge you would rather avoid than engage might be right around the corner.

Manage your mindset. It is yours to control. Use it to your advantage because it is a terrible thing to waste.

---

[1] Viktor Frankl, *Man's Search for Meaning*, trans. Ilse Lasch (Boston: Beacon Press, 1959), 66.

Chapter Five

Leaving Work

"Have we told you about the fast and slow ways to lose your job here?" asked Tom as he sat in his office with Chuck and Eric. It was 1984, my first year in the corporate world as a marketing research analyst at Quaker Oats. Since they each had two to three years more experience than me, the answer was easy.

"No," I replied, excited that these mentor-bosses were about to share a secret certain to advance my career.

I leaned forward as they began tag-teaming their way through their latest version of how the "fast way" might unfold.

"It starts like this. You're having a bad day—could be for any number of reasons. . . . Maybe it's work; maybe something going on at home. . . . Either way, you step out of your cubicle and head down the second floor hallway toward the cafeteria. The walk won't take long; it's only about one hundred yards. . . . At the end of the corridor is an open stairway. Climb up to the third floor. . . . Straight ahead, you'll see the door to the CEO's office. . . . A security guard will be posted there. . . . Say hello and tell him you have an appointment. . . . Stay calm. But don't hesitate. Move decisively. . . . Inside, the administrative assistant will be seated at her desk. Walk past her, too. She'll try to slow you down by asking your name. Ignore her request. . . . Go right to the CEO's door, and enter. Don't bother knocking. . . . Inside you'll spot him seated behind a desk the size of a tennis court."

I was beginning to wonder if they might be embellishing a bit on the specifics, but the serious clarity with which my friends spoke led me to believe this might have actually happened to one of their former colleagues.

"Stand there until the CEO looks up. When he does, walk straight to his desk. . . . Pause for a brief moment to make sure he is listening. Then pound your fist on the desktop and declare: 'This place is really screwed up and let me tell you why!' . . . Here's where you get to improvise a bit. But not too much. Just a couple sentences that put some reasonably relevant meat on your bones of discontent. . . . Once you've had your say, turn and make a quick exit. Don't look back. . . . What is done is done. Keep moving forward."

By now, I knew this was a bad plan headed for a worse finale. But as Tom, Chuck, and Eric took turns building the scene, the pace of their play-by-play account quickened.

"Here's where it gets interesting. . . . Make your exit. Again, don't look back. Keep moving forward. What is done is done. . . . Head toward the stairway. By the time you reach the bottom step, the guard will have called the security office, reporting the name on your badge. . . . As you start down the hallway, they will be phoning your supervisor. By the time you reach the restrooms and you're about halfway back, the head of our department will be cleaning out your desk. . . . When you turn the last corner, he'll be standing there with a cardboard box holding all of your personal belongings. . . . No words will be exchanged. Only the box. . . . The guard who had been following you will ask you to hand over your ID badge. A second guard will join him. They'll grab you under each arm and escort you out the back door. That, Larry, is the fast way to get fired here!"

It had taken Tom, Chuck, and Eric at least five minutes to delineate the details of this rapid exit strategy. It was clear that they had shared this sequence of events many times before, but hearing it for the first time, I was left with an obvious question: "If that's the fast way, what's the slow way to get fired here?"

Chuck and Eric looked toward Tom, who appeared to be in deep thought as he reflected on my question. After a short pause, which I now realize was mostly for effect, Tom said, "That's simple. You just stop doing your job."

"What?" I asked.

Tom explained that once you had established yourself as a competent and dependable employee, you qualified for a most coveted job perk—immense leeway from your bosses. "They'll take it upon themselves to explain away your performance lapses with comments like 'He's just having a bad day' or 'He'll come out of it in time,'" Tom continued. "Depending on how well you play this work-stoppage ploy, it could take weeks, even months, for them to truly notice the obvious pattern of un-performance. And here's the best part: the more positive annual performance appraisals human resources have on file before you stop doing your job, the longer it might take for them to figure it out."

***

Almost twenty-five years later, I slipped into my own version of the "slow way" to leave a job. But mine reversed the roles imagined by my former colleagues. Instead of me deciding to no longer do my job, the company I had worked at for thirteen years stopped asking me to work in areas I considered to be my core competencies.

I didn't see it coming. My career had gone well for more than twenty years, at least as measured by outward signs such as an impressive title, a nice compensation package, a corner office, a calendar overpopulated with meetings. Although our corporate sales had weakened a bit, they were still positive, and the future looked promising. The first inkling of trouble appeared during my annual performance appraisal, when my supervisor said, "I gave you a positive review, Larry. I'm not sure if that will be good or bad for you."

Within a week of delivering these cryptic words, he was gone, and I was left with a mysterious dark cloud hanging over my head. Six months later, my responsibilities were reduced by half. When I met with the president to discuss how I thought I was being underutilized, he suggested the move was "in the best interests of the company"—one of those phrases that carries sufficient ambiguous weight to avoid challenge. He recommended I focus on my remaining role, but within six months, members of the small innovation team I led became victims of the latest reduction in force. I was assigned a final position that seemed, at the time, to offer no future. My career had been routed onto a lonely off-ramp.

I had witnessed a lot of people leave companies during my career, enough to crack the code on the language used to describe the circumstances. "To pursue other interests" suggested the decision had been made by the company; "To take (*insert specific job or company here*)" meant the employee had decided. My exit didn't fit either model. There was no organizational announcement, no fanfare. On my last day I walked out the door carrying a cardboard box containing my personal belongings. At least I had ample time to pack it myself.

In the weeks and months ahead, I discovered how difficult it can be to move on. My sense of self-worth had gotten so tightly wound into my career that I wondered who I was now. I found it easy to blame others for perceived slights. I became fixated on events from the past, on those I felt had done me wrong, pondering what "could have been" instead of planning where to go next. Left to my own devices, I was happy to hold on to the past and blame others for my declining self-regard.

I wasn't proud of the fact that history was still nipping at my heels, following me wherever I went. I felt disappointment with my obvious lack of resiliency. Then, a few months later, I noticed the safety warning on the passenger-side mirror of my car that read: "Objects in the mirror are closer than they appear." In that moment, I realized that holding on to perceived slights from my past was having the opposite effect. I was allowing events behind me to loom larger than they should have been by now. I needed to find some way to do what the mirror did—reduce those images from the past into something smaller and more distant—because if I kept looking back, I would never be able to see all the possibilities that lay ahead of me.

***

In his November 2012 TED talk, teacher Phuc Tran shared how growing up in the US with his Vietnamese parents shaped his identity. Tran attributed his father's positive orientation in the face of life's difficulties to the absence of the subjunctive form (using a verb to express a wish, desire, hope, or possibility) in his native Vietnamese language.[1] According to Tran, his father was unable to express regrets because Vietnamese possessed no ways by which he could speak them. While some critics have challenged the underlying premise that people cannot think in ways their language does not support (called the Sapir-Whorf hypothesis), the concept offered a mechanism I could use to move my thinking away from a sense of disappointment I had hung on to for far too long. By banning the use of subjunctive form to describe nonfactual action related to my situation—such as "I should have" or "I wish I had"—I steered my reflections in a more positive, action-oriented direction and became better able to live in the present.

My "slow way" out of my career had become an impediment to moving forward because I'd allowed it to be one. I realized those who I blamed were not losing any sleep over the past (and probably never did), so why was I? Worse, I was doing what all who hold a grudge end up doing: carrying all the weight of it. By eliminating the "what if" or "I should have" thoughts about my final year of corporate life, I was able to fully appreciate the positive twenty-four years that preceded it and, by extension, my entire career.

Emotions, especially negative ones, will find a way to resurface until we give them the attention and the respect they deserve. The best way to channel them into something positive is to embrace them head on, make friends with them, and recognize how you changed and grew as a result. Reframing my history allowed me to savor the best, scrap the rest, and find a path forward.

***

I now realize there was practical wisdom buried in Tom, Chuck, and Eric's fictional depiction of the way to leave an organization. They had said, "Make a quick exit. Don't look back. . . . What is done is done. Keep moving forward." Sound advice I wish I would have taken years later when I had the chance.

---

[1] "Grammar, Identity, and the Dark Side of the Subjunctive: Phuc Tran at TEDxDirigo," TEDx Talks, November 26, 2012, YouTube, accessed May 15, 2023, https://www.youtube.com/watch?v=zeSVMG4GkeQ.

Chapter Six

A Peek through the Curtain

I did not intend to eavesdrop on the private moments of a celebrity. It just happened. While my view through the black sheer curtain was far from perfect that evening, it offered an insightful glimpse into what contributed to one man's long and successful career.

Noel Stookey, better known as "Paul" of the trio Peter, Paul, and Mary, played a key role in the American folk music revival in the 1960s. I listened to their recordings in my youth, marveling at Noel's ability to find that third harmony note that perfectly complemented his bandmates' voices. His playful persona expressed through extended monologues lent a lighthearted touch to serious matters of social justice. Noel is, without a doubt, a folk icon.

As part of the legendary ensemble and as a solo artist, Noel recorded over forty albums. His work was always guided by a core belief that music can be a vehicle for raising awareness and consciousness of the pressing social and political issues of the day. Noel's best-known composition, "The Wedding Song (There is Love)," was his wedding gift to trio member Peter Yarrow. Royalties from sales go to the Public Domain Foundation, where nearly $2 million has been put to work in support of charitable causes.

Responding to an invitation from Jim Newton, founder of a not-for-profit organization now named KidLinks,[1] Noel agreed to help produce songs intended to bring healing and emotional support to severely ill children and their caregivers. These KidLinks songs were crafted with intentional messages these suffering little ones need to hear. Noel expected his role would be limited to providing advice from a distance and endorsing their work. Impressed with both the quality of the initial compositions and Newton's passion for his therapeutic music mission, Noel joined the team in 1986 to contribute his talent and experience to composing songs and producing multiple award-winning children's recordings. He summed up his experience with KidLinks and its mission in this way when I interviewed him a few years ago:

We have learned a lot about what the core mission of KidLinks is. It's not about just making music. It's not about being successful in the world's eyes. It is about keeping your anchor line tied to the original premise of making a difference in a child's life.

I had been volunteering with KidLinks as a therapeutic musician for almost three years, visiting children at local hospitals to offer helpful and healing songs, when Jim asked me to join him and his musical partner, Paul G. Hill, on a road trip to Houston in 2013. Noel was coming to Texas to perform two concerts to raise funds for KidLinks, the first at an Irish pub in Houston and a second the following evening in Dallas. I was delighted to accept Jim's invitation, even if it meant roadie duty hauling guitars and lifting luggage. My reward would be a prime seat at Noel's concert.

When that day arrived, Jim, Paul, and I played our guitars and sang at Children's Memorial Hermann Hospital in Houston before heading to the airport to pick up Noel. The schedule for the afternoon was straightforward:

- 2:00 - Pick up Noel at George Bush Intercontinental Airport

- 4:00 - Early Dinner (location TBD)

- 5:00 - Arrive at McGonigel's Mucky Duck for sound check

- 6:00 - VIP Guest Reception with Noel

- 7:00 - Private Time for Noel

- 8:00 - Concert Start

I paced back and forth in the baggage area as we waited for Noel's flight to arrive. I had met a few famous people in my life but had never had the chance to hang out with the star long enough to get beyond surface chitchat. I had no idea what I might find in common with a celebrity like Noel, but the moment I saw his towering frame and shook his impressive hand for the first time, my uneasiness vanished.

"Hello, Larry," he said. "I've heard good things about you from Jim." His vivid blue eyes exuded warmth that underscored the genuineness of his words.

After our early dinner, we arrived at McGonigel's, where I began my assignment of selling Noel's latest CD recording as guests arrived for the VIP reception. I was stationed in the hallway outside a cozy room that served as a library, wine cellar, and performer greenroom, depending on the need. I marveled at how Noel greeted each visitor with the same positive regard he had bestowed upon me. He shook their hands and posed for photos. Conversations that echoed from the space to where I stood evoked the feel of a long-awaited reunion of friends, not a paid-for meet and greet.

When the last guests exited the room at 7:00 p.m., I imagined Noel must have felt exhausted. "And he still has a couple hours of performing ahead of him," I thought. As the double French doors closed, leaving Noel alone for the first time in hours, I expected the lights to dim as he took time out for some preconcert ritual designed to center himself and collect his thoughts. As I peered through the sheer curtains, I watched Noel pull a guitar from its case and begin to play the same sequence of chords over and over again, working on timing and developing the digital muscle memory only repetition can produce. He continued for more than forty-five minutes, stopping just a couple of moments before taking the stage.

I cannot overstate the positive impression the scene made on me. I recall thinking, "Here is a genuine folk icon . . . a real star . . . someone who has performed in front of large audiences . . . on some of the world's grandest stages . . . during a career spanning over half a century . . . with an hour for himself prior to a small charitable event . . . having the freedom to do anything he wants . . . and he is *practicing*!"

Our true character is revealed by what we do when no one is watching. In that moment, I learned more about Noel "Paul" Stookey than any account others could provide me. I saw him as more than a folk music star. I bore witness to a man unwilling to rest on his notoriety or past successes. I beheld a celebrity dedicated to getting better at the craft of music that brought him fame. I recognized a talented man demanding the best from himself because he understood that was what his audience deserved.

In his bestseller *Outliers: The Story of Success*, Malcolm Gladwell popularized the idea that ten thousand hours of deliberate practice can lead to world-class expertise in any skill. While some critics have suggested this "rule" is an oversimplification because it fails to consider other factors such as innate talent, there is little doubt that working your craft twenty hours a week for ten years will make you pretty good at it. That is what makes Noel "Paul" Stookey's use of the "personal time" on his itinerary to log one more hour of practice so impressive. Multiply the ten-thousand-hour magic number by six, and you get a reasonable estimate of how many hours Noel had already dedicated to his craft.[2]

Before that evening, I thought I knew what it meant to dedicate myself to getting better at something. But as I peeked through the veil of that black curtain, Noel reframed what it meant to *commit to excellence*. Even though he had been performing for over fifty years and was well past the age of seventy, there was Noel, working to sharpen his art and deliver the best performance he could.

Some people, likely the most successful ones, never allow themselves to rest on their laurels. Perhaps that is what makes them worthy of our admiration.

[1] *Music on a Mission: The KidLinks Story* (2022) by Larry Dykstra provides more information about KidLinks. This book covers the history of a nonprofit organization that emerged out of unexpected origins and overcame countless challenges to provide the power of music for children in need for forty years and counting. It is a story of how one's passionate pursuit of a clearly defined purpose can make a life-changing difference in the lives of those one serves.
[2] 20 hours a week x 60 years = over 60,000 hours

Chapter Seven

We Pay You to Talk

I suspect he laid his eyes on me long before I spotted him through the drizzle and gloom of the Northern California night. A silhouette at first, but as he neared, I could see he wore layers of ragged clothing chosen to protect him during nights on the streets. I dreaded the encounter ahead.

If you have ever lived in or traveled to a large city, chances are you are familiar with that uneasy feeling inside when a homeless person approaches. As much as we would like to believe we are willing to help anyone in need, that aspirational depiction of our nature can vanish in an instant when we meet face to face with a person of the streets. That was how it was for me as I walked in the darkness back to my hotel near downtown San Francisco. My sole interest became navigating past an oncoming stranger.

We were about ten feet from each other when he stopped in his tracks. "Here it comes," I thought, expecting to receive a pitch for a dollar or two honed through years of practice. But a puzzled look crossed his face before he paused, smiled, and declared, "Man, your shirt is really f***ed up!"

I knew he spoke the truth. A gray cotton-wool-blend turtleneck drooped and sagged below my chin like a worn-out dishrag. I had realized it was not the height of fashion when I'd donned it before heading out to dinner, but I'd assumed no one would notice, much less say anything about it. I had become attached to that shirt despite undeniable flaws I no longer acknowledged. It took that homeless gentleman with nothing to gain (and perhaps a few dollars to lose) to give me the straight truth. His feedback was clear and authentic, which also made it actionable. I took off the shirt the moment I returned to my hotel room, then left it behind for housekeeping to dispose of however they saw fit.

A homeless stranger's critique of my wardrobe was the second-best personal feedback I ever received. Gold medal in this category goes to the head of human resources at the Fortune 500 company where we worked together for years. I had helped Joe with a couple of corporate culture-building initiatives, so I suspected he was bringing a similar assignment when he arrived unannounced at my office one day. After I invited him in, Joe sat across from me and got right to the point. "We pay you to talk in meetings."

My back stiffened as visions of a corporate career lost flashed through my mind.

Joe's feedback was unambiguous and authentic. He didn't sugarcoat the message using the "but sandwich" framework his department had trained us to use when presenting developmental opportunities to our direct reports. (It goes like this: "What I appreciate about you is [insert a couple of positive comments], but you could be more effective if you [suggest areas for improvement].") No. Joe gave it to me straight, launching me on what would be the most useful coaching process of my career.

I am not sure what precipitated Joe's visit that day. I suspect it was not any particular incident but rather a pattern of behavior that raised concerns about my apparent reticence to share points of view on the matters under discussion. In hindsight, I could envision plenty of times during my twenty-five-year business career and personal life when I may have left colleagues and friends wondering, "Where does Larry stand on this issue?" Joe's feedback opened my eyes to the fact that my silence spoke volumes.

For introverts like me, it is easy to chalk up our communication inadequacies (particularly in situations where the discussion is moving fast) as a reflection of our true selves, not as a developmental issue. We have received support for this view over the past years with best-selling books like *Quiet: The Power of Introverts in a World That Can't Stop Talking*, by Susan Cain.[1] The book's subtitle signals that the author makes the case for how personality tendencies like mine are undervalued in organizations run by hard-charging and vocal extroverts. According to Cain, introverts add unique value through our strengths of listening, self-awareness, introspection, and creativity. That's certainly how I saw it.

That was also how Hollywood portrayed under communicating in the 1979 movie *Being There*. Peter Sellers starred in the role of Chance, a simpleminded servant who spent years tending to the garden of a wealthy gentleman in Washington, DC. When he wanders into the outside world, his simple comments are interpreted as profound insights into matters of public policy. The ambiguity of his commentary is not only misinterpreted but rewarded. In time, Chance becomes regarded as a wise political expert who becomes adviser to the president. While that makes for a great story, inadequate communication does not work that way in the real world.

I am thankful to Joe for piercing through my shield of silence with a message so clear and direct that I could not ignore it. More impressive was the way he backed up his feedback with resources designed to define my personality characteristics and identify my preferred management styles and work environments. Reflecting on this new information helped me identify self-imposed governors on speaking and potential solutions I could implement to overcome them.

I discovered that I might be slow to speak in meetings because I was still in the process of developing my point of view, a challenge shared by most introverts who feel the need to think through their response before sharing. In my case, I was spending so much time searching for the evidence to support an opinion that I missed the opportunity to deliver one. To address my hesitancy, I started to lean on years of experience to support my intuitions rather than rethink each problem anew. I began to caveat my thoughts by starting with, "I haven't completely thought this through, but my initial reaction is . . ." This was a way to give myself permission to offer a view without waiting until I reached the point of certainty.

I also discovered one nasty side effect of a delayed response was that by the time I reached a point of view, the moment to share it had passed. I resolved that if the matter was important enough, it was okay to return the discussion to an earlier topic by saying something like, "I'm sorry, but can we go back to the issue we just discussed?" I found that teammates willingly accepted this approach if something of value came from the detour.

A more subtle insight that came out of this process was the realization that on many occasions, I remained silent because I felt my opinion had already been expressed by others. In those moments, my failure to comment might have signaled I was not in agreement with what had already been said. I needed to send some message of agreement, either by nodding or simply repeating what had been said by others in my own words. Lacking this kind of overt feedback from me, my colleagues may have assumed I wasn't with them.

A popular idiom states, "Nature abhors a vacuum." The same notion applies to humans when it comes to communication. The silence of unspoken words leaves a space others feel a need to fill, revealing this core truth: lacking information from you, others will fill in the gaps for themselves. More importantly, they might default to a negative narrative. I saw that my silence spoke volumes, expressing messages I neither possessed nor intended. Now I understand that since no one can read my mind, it is my responsibility to replace the ambiguity my silence created and *fill the gaps* with the clarity of my own words.

That is why I so value the best two pieces of feedback I received in my life, one from a homeless stranger and the other from an experienced human resources colleague. Despite the vast differences between their backgrounds and our relationships, both communicated in a way all constructive feedback should be shared. They were authentic messengers who were also concise, using only seven words each. Their words contained no gaps for me to fill in on my own, only actions to take.

---

[1] Susan Cain, *Quiet: The Power of Introverts in a World That Can't Stop Talking* (New York City, NY: Crown Publishing Group, 2013).

Chapter Eight

Put Your Own Mask on First

Seven of us joined the program with a shared desire to use our musical gifts to serve others. On this day we would each get a chance to apply eighty hours of classroom learning into twenty minutes of what we hoped would be healing music for our first patients.

During my first year of retirement, I developed a strong interest in how music could be used as a healing modality. To complement what I was learning as a volunteer with the KidLinks organization, I entered the Music for Healing and Transition Program (MHTP) being offered for the first time in the Dallas area. The MHTP curriculum consisted of eighty hours of class instruction and outside readings designed to prepare musicians for providing live therapeutic music at the bedsides of the sick and the dying as well as for those who care for them. MHTP seemed like the perfect way to gain insight into the realities of playing music for others in hospitals. On this practicum day, I was treated to an experience more powerful than I could have ever imagined.

As we huddled in the foyer of a children's hospital, our instructor announced the assignments: "Larry, you will be playing for Jason, a seventeen-year-old male who is in a coma. He is awake, agitated, but unresponsive." I felt confused. I could understand how a comatose patient might be "unresponsive," but nothing else in Beth's description fit the soap opera image of a peacefully sleeping patient. I had played and sung countless times to four-year-old children at the day care center where I worked, but this was uncharted territory.

There was little time for worry to set in. A few moments later, Beth and I entered Jason's room, where I found him seated and facing away from the door. Walls were decorated with posters of his favorite college team, along with countless get-well cards and balloons. It was clear he had been here for quite some time.

Jason's father stood hunched in front of his son, trying to feed him. His father encouraged him to take a drink, but Jason did not respond to his prompts. The man rattled the cup inches from his son's face, much like you might shake a toy in front of a pet's nose, hoping to capture his attention. Finally, Jason took a small sip through the straw.

I asked the father if it would be all right if I provided some music, and, after an uncomfortable pause, he agreed. I sensed he was not excited at the presence of two total strangers in his son's room.

I moved to the center of the room and turned to face Jason. He gripped the arms of his wheelchair, as if holding on for dear life. His legs jerked about; a seat belt was the only thing keeping him restrained. I asked if I could sing to him, but Jason continued his vacant stare toward the floor. I made eye contact with his father, who had moved to the corner of the room. He nodded his approval.

I eased into a familiar ballad, knowing I could adjust depending on Jason's response. The opening G chord resonated louder than I expected throughout the small room and grabbed Jason's attention. His gaze moved a bit higher, focused on my playing hand as I sang the first verse and chorus.

A couple of minutes later I began to hum the tune, and Jason raised his chin away from his chest. A wide smile crossed his face, one that made me feel like I was a long-lost friend he had rediscovered. When I struck a misshapen chord, Jason chuckled at my clumsy technique. As I neared the end of the song, he brought his hands together like one might while saying a prayer and looked me in the eye, as if he was trying to say, "Thank you." With each new verse, Jason had become more engaged in the music and the world around him. I felt like I was participating in an unimaginable miracle.

I played a second song but recall little about it. Sensing I might be nearing my twenty-minute limit, I decided to end the session. When I bowed to thank Jason for the opportunity to play for him, his body was relaxed and still. No more moving, no more shifting, no kicking. Jason was at peace.

I left his room and made it no farther than the hallway before I broke into tears. My initial sadness at the sight of this ailing young man had morphed into awe at his response to my music. Beth placed a comforting arm around me and said, "You were meant to be here."

***

Later that afternoon, my classmates and I shared our experiences playing to patients. When the discussion moved to the tasks we needed to complete before the final phase of the program, a forty-hour internship, I spoke to the more pressing concern on my mind: "What can I do for Jason now?"

"You might be able to arrange an internship at his hospital," said our instructor, Beth, "but you must pass the final exam before that can begin."

This felt more like an obstacle than a requirement. "Why can't I go back and play for him sooner?" I asked.

"You're not ready," said Beth.

"But the music had a positive impact today. Maybe it would be stronger next time and would be a real help to him," I said, continuing to plead my case.

"There's just no way to make it happen," she explained. "You made a difference when you played for Jason, but you can't afford to think you can save him. That's up to God and Jason.

What if you remain wrapped up in helping him and he dies anyway? Where will your emotions be then?"

I felt like challenging the process, but there was no way to argue with this voice of reason. Beth was right: I lacked the experience an internship would provide.

When I studied my calendar later that evening, reality sank in. Due to an upcoming trip to Turkey to see my wife, Sandy, who was fulfilling a four-month teaching assignment there, the approaching holidays, and the program requirements I needed to complete, the earliest I might begin an internship was months away. I accepted the reality that playing again for Jason would never happen.

***

I was packing for Turkey a couple of weeks later when the phone rang. It was Beth. "Can you meet me at the hospital this afternoon?" she asked.

"I leave for my trip tomorrow," I replied, avoiding a premature commitment. "Why? What's up?"

"I can't tell you over the phone, but it's important that you meet me here today if you can make it. Can you meet me at the labyrinth outside the hospital at one p.m.?"

"Sure, Beth. I'll see you then."

"Great, Larry. Oh, and bring your guitar."

When I met Beth at the labyrinth, she explained Jason's condition had deteriorated and he had been placed on a ventilator. The machines supporting his life had been removed that morning. Searching for anything that might help Jason after this critical procedure, his father had recalled my initial visit and asked whether I could return.

Beth said it was time to see Jason, so I grabbed my guitar and followed her into the hospital. A short elevator ride brought us to a hallway painted an institutional green color—a stark contrast to the cheerful decor at the children's facility where I'd first met Jason a couple of weeks before. After a short walk, Beth stopped in front of a door. "This is his room. Don't be alarmed by what you see."

Inside, I saw Jason lying on his right side, facing the door. I scanned the room and recognized the father standing to my right, shifting stiffly in position. A woman who I assumed to be his mother reclined behind him, supporting his body while stroking his shoulder and arm. Recalling Jason's condition during my initial visit, I took mental inventory. Yes, he was still comatose. No, he was no longer awake or agitated. The only movement was his chest, which heaved and fell in no pattern or rhythm.

I leaned in and asked Jason if it was okay for me to play a song. He did not respond. I glanced at the monitor and noted his elevated and erratic pulse. I took a deep breath and began strumming my guitar at a consistent sixty beats per minute, hoping this tempo would help regulate Jason's breathing and heartbeat.[1] But Jason continued to gasp and gulp for air, each breath a struggle. I added humming, then vocals. I scanned the monitors again, hoping to see some sign of response. Nothing had changed.

After twenty minutes, maybe more, I wondered how much longer I should play. To continue seemed pointless. Seeing this young life so full of potential reduced to a series of numbers and patterns illuminated on a digital monitor broke my heart and my resolve. I strummed one last chord, took a step closer to his bed, and whispered, "Goodbye, Jason. God be with you."

***

The next morning, I began my trip to Turkey. During a layover in New York's JFK Airport, I found refuge in a quiet waiting area where I could finish the last two chapters of *Music as Medicine*, music therapist Deforia Lane's account of her life of music, healing, and faith.[2] Sitting alone, I read her story about a comatose patient with terminal cancer. While doctors concluded nothing could be done, a devoted friend played music on their dulcimer at his bedside every day until, to everyone's surprise, he awoke from the coma. Later, that patient described how the sounds entered his brain and stirred within him the desire to find the music.

Through this story, I glimpsed what might have been happening on Jason's end while I sang to him the day before. Despite the lack of a visible response, maybe he had heard the music and it had given him a reason to fight for life. I could see how helping Jason simply required commitment, patience, and time. I promised I would find a way to return to Jason's room following my three weeks abroad to provide a musical tug that would penetrate his coma-muddled world and bring him back to his family and friends.

Realizing my flight to Istanbul would be boarding soon, I organized my belongings before heading to the departure gate. Checking messages on my cell phone one last time, I noticed a missed call from Beth. Her message was brief: "Jason passed away this afternoon, surrounded by his family. I thought you would want to know."

Emotions now pulled in so many directions—I didn't know how to respond to Beth's message. I just took my place in the queue and boarded the plane, wishing it might somehow carry me far away from my sadness.

***

A few minutes later, after settling into my window seat, I tried to find some meaning in this latest twist in my mission to bring music and healing to Jason. I didn't have to wait long. During the standard preflight announcements, a flight attendant spoke familiar words I heard in a whole new way: "In case of an emergency, always put your own mask on first."

In that moment, I saw my two visits with Jason in a different light. What had started out as a practicum in therapeutic music had brought me face to face with the issue my instructor, Beth, had warned me about after my initial visit with Jason: getting too attached to our patients and their outcomes carries the risk of burning out.

There is a line separating *caring* from *caring too much* that is difficult to see. So, whether you are tending to the needs of a friend, your child, or a parent, always bear in mind this lesson that might be called the *paradox of caring*: you can attend to the needs of others only if you take care of yourself first.

---

[1] *Entrainment* is a phenomenon where the signal frequency of one system's motion impacts another system, leading it to adopt the same frequency. The most common example is when pendulum clocks near each other will synchronize their movement. The application here is that in the presence of a guitar strummed at a consistent sixty beats per minute, a patient's heart will adapt to or entrain to the same rhythm.
[2] Deforia Lane and Rob Wilkins, *Music as Medicine* (Grand Rapids: Zandervan, 1996).

Summary of Part I

Lessons I Have Learned from my Relationship with Self

- ➢ Keep learning, adjusting, and growing. What determines success changes with time, and so must you.

- ➢ Pursue your passion. Loving what you do helps cut through the drudgery and keep you going over the long haul.

- ➢ Bark less, wag more. A smile has the potential to benefit giver and receiver alike.

- ➢ Manage your mindset. It is yours to control, so use it to your advantage.

- ➢ Move forward. If you keep looking back and asking "What if?", you will miss the possibilities that lie ahead.

- ➢ Commit to excellence. Successful people never allow themselves to rest on their laurels.

- ➢ Fill the gaps. Replace the ambiguity of silence with the clarity of your words.

- ➢ Take care of yourself. Self-care is the prerequisite for being able to attend to the needs of others.

Part II: Others

When I was a freshman in college in the early 1970s, a wall of just about every dorm room was decorated with the same poster. I'm not talking about ones picturing Farrah Fawcett in a swimsuit or rock legends like the Who or Led Zeppelin. Imagine instead the deep-blue sky above a churning sea, framing a tiny body of land in the far distance. Printed over the scene in white letters is this universal truth by English poet John Donne:

No man is an island, entire of itself.

At the time, I considered the popularity of Donne's wisdom a sign of a growing maturity that arrives around the time the first digit of our age changes from one to two. When we set off on our own, it doesn't take long to realize we do not travel through this world alone. We begin to recognize a circle of interdependence exists, that our actions impact others and their actions impact ours.

I turn now to stories about people and events that helped me understand how to be more effective in my relationships with others. In most cases, there was nothing grand or earthshaking that precipitated the action. Instead, the road into these tales was paved by paying attention to the ways in which I was treated, by observing the actions of role models and leaders, by knowing what it is like to be there for someone in need, by noticing what happens when asking others for help, or by trying to walk in somebody else's shoes.

Chapter Nine

A Seven-Minute Struggle

Less than two minutes into the experiment, I was ready to quit. But I realized my father did not have that option. He lived each day with the limitation I had artificially forced upon myself—to dress without the use of my left arm.

My dad was as active as anyone in their eighties could hope to be. He loved outdoor tasks such as mowing his large lawn or trimming the evergreen hedges. These activities offered a sense of accomplishment and management of nature, both meaningful to a lifelong farmer. Following his retirement, he discovered the game of golf and walked all eighteen holes on the course he played two or three times each week. His natural athletic ability enabled him to regularly score around ninety strokes—not bad for a man in his eighties. At the rate he was going, his average score per round was on track to reach a number lower than his age.

But after his ninetieth birthday, a stroke of the most vicious kind took away that possibility. His left side suffered major damage. "It's dead," he told me after the event, pointing to that arm as it hung like a limp rag by his side. The stroke had taken a toll on his body in terms of strength, mobility, and balance. When his physical therapist asked about his goals, Dad said, "I'd like to golf again."

"I'm not going to mislead you, Ralph. It's not gonna happen," replied the therapist, sending a message that reset expectations.

While I was visiting Dad in the hospital, a language therapist came to his room to test his cognitive skills with a word-generation exercise we have all played at some time. "Look at the word printed on the top of the page," she said, "and write down as many three-or-more-letter words you can think of using only the letters in that word." The word was *restaurant.*

Dad grabbed the pen and, without hesitation, wrote *truant* on the first line. The therapist and I looked at each other and shook our heads in amazement. He didn't go for the obvious answers like *rest* or *ant* or *rant.* Dad went for what was perhaps the least obvious one. "No problems upstairs," I thought to myself. The stroke that had sentenced his body to physical therapy had pardoned his memory and left intact cognitive abilities as acute as those of a person half his age.

Weeks of rehabilitation in the hospital improved his mobility and balance to a level where he could return home. Dad would need help with many activities of daily living (termed ADLs by occupational therapists) such as bathing, grooming, and dressing. My mom, a devoted wife and career nurse, was eager to assist. This partnership would be critical if they were to continue living independently in the comfort of the home they had built and lived in together for over four decades.

Through determination and the help of a sidestepper (a four-legged walker that resembles a small stepladder), Dad used the remaining strength on his right side to navigate around their one-story home. Mom managed daily life back to a new normal, delivering snacks as he sat in his favorite chair, setting out his medications, and helping him bathe.

But I never heard discussion about how Dad dressed himself. I assumed Mom played a supporting role here as well, but it was never mentioned. That is why I found my brother Curt's suggestion so profound in its simplicity: "Try dressing yourself without the use of your left arm," he said. After a couple of weeks of procrastination, I endeavored to do just that.

I closed the bathroom door, stripped off my clothes, laid them neatly across the floor, and started the stopwatch. Donning my underpants was the first task. I found it easy to get the briefs positioned around my ankles, but as I was pulling the shorts up to my waist, I caught myself leaning against the wall for support. Given my dad's uncertain balance and weakness in his left leg, I wondered if he had that luxury. I knew he didn't.

The undershirt posed a greater challenge. As it hung loosely from my right hand, I was uncertain how to best orient the garment to initiate the process. I decided grabbing the shirt by its tail might be a good place to start. Holding it upside down, I pulled the shirt's left sleeve up and over my dangling arm. Once it was inserted, I was able to pull the shirt over my head and then elevate the right arm into its sleeve. Following numerous tugs and pulls to position it correctly around my waistline, the undershirt was in place.

The task of putting on the long-sleeved shirt came next. Within a few seconds, far faster than I had anticipated, the shirt was draped around my shoulders with both arms inserted into their proper sleeves. That was when the trouble began. Buttons have been around for centuries, and it is easy to take for granted our capacity to make these fasteners work. I won't make that mistake again. The buttonhole and button resisted each other like a pair of bratty children refusing to play together. After a full minute of awkward fumbling, I succeeded in getting the first pair to engage. The second button found a partner much faster, as did the third, leading me to believe I was getting the hang of this docking maneuver. But the shirt hung unevenly because the alignment was off by one buttonhole, forcing me to undo the three secured buttons and start over again. The thought of giving up revisited my mind, but I pushed it aside with the realization that Dad didn't have that option. He never would.

Putting on my pants was easier than expected, but I found tucking the shirt into the waistline demanded an iterative series of pushes and pulls that required time and patience. I didn't bother trying to put on the belt, a clear sign that my tolerance with this self-imposed dressing challenge was wearing thin. "I bet Mom does that for him," I thought, excusing myself from this step and remembering again how critical her assistance must be in the small details of his daily life.

After adding socks and slipping into a pair of loafers, I considered myself "dressed." The timer on my stopwatch read just under seven minutes—the time it takes for me to walk almost a half mile.

This exercise in empathy made just one of the challenges my father faced—getting dressed—both visceral and personal. I realized how little I understood about the daily difficulties he accepted without complaint. I came away with a much deeper appreciation for how much my father depended on my mother and the enormous pride coupled with weariness that she must have felt by helping him through the activities of daily life that used to be second nature. I saw how his physical limits fed her emotional purpose in an impressive testament to the enduring power of the wedding vows Ralph and Alice Dykstra had made to each other more than seventy years ago.

Struggling for seven minutes to dress myself without the use of one arm made me realize that we can never understand the frustration and pain others endure unless we try to make it personal. In those moments when it is difficult to appreciate why someone else—an employee, boss, child, partner, or friend—is feeling and acting in ways we don't fully understand, it is important to move beyond thinking "What's their deal?" to asking "What do I need to understand about what is causing him to act this way?" Answering that question may require you to put on their robe, place your feet into their slippers, maybe even shuffle a half mile or more in them, and *let empathy be your teacher.*

Chapter Ten

The Verbatim Report

You can learn a lot about how to perform a skill by observing someone who is genuinely bad at it. That is one of the many things I learned during my graduate studies from reading masterful books by Yale professor Edward Tufte, a thought leader in the field of information design. His multiple publications contained rare statistical graphics, charts, and reports that illustrate best practices when communicating information in a compelling manner. But in his book *Visual Explanations*, Tufte flipped the script when he suggested that studying the craft of magic can offer insight into *what to avoid* when presenting content because the magician's goal is to mislead the audience through what he termed "disinformation design."[1]

As much as I liked Professor Tufte's perspective on how insight can be gained from studying "worst practices," I had never found a clear application until I recently spent time with my friend Jacob. I used to look forward to reunions, when we could reminisce about the past and catch up on what was new in our lives. But over the years our talks drifted into lopsided contests where every comment I made elicited a sort of homing pigeon effect—Jacob countered with a connection back to *his* family, *his* career, *his* favorite sports team, or *his* latest physical ailment. When I spoke, the vacant look in his eyes indicated he was too busy working out his next comment to hear anything I said. If I was telling a story, he might interrupt with what he considered a better one. I stopped volunteering to give information about myself because I knew exactly where any topic would lead: right back to him and his world. In time, I concluded our reunions weren't worth it anymore. What is the point in hanging out with someone who is interested only in himself?

***

My friend's extreme case of poor listening practices contributed to my belief that I was somehow good at the role. However, my understanding of what is required of an effective listener was transformed during the eight months I served as a chaplain in a children's hospital. It was a casual comment over lunch with a pastor at my church, Kathleen, that opened my eyes to the possibility of serving as a chaplain. When I mentioned my volunteer work in the hospital as a therapeutic musician, Kathleen asked, "Have you ever thought about CPE?"

"What is that?" I asked, with no idea what the initials stood for. Kathleen explained that CPE, or clinical pastoral education, was a form of theological education that took place in clinical settings, typically hospitals. She told me that most seminaries required students to complete one unit of CPE (one hundred hours of study, three hundred hours of clinical experience) before graduation. However, several laypersons also participated. "You should consider it, Larry," she concluded. "After all, you're already going to the hospital." I applied and was accepted for an extended unit of CPE that would run from September 2012 through April 2013.

The model of learning used in CPE encouraged me and my peers to interact with patients and their caregivers and then reflect on our actions to gain a deeper understanding of their needs and how effective we were at addressing them. This approach facilitated rapid growth and personal learning about oneself in the role of a practicing caregiver, with listening skills as a key dimension.

One tool used in CPE training is the verbatim report, where a chaplain documents an encounter with a patient, a parent, a staff member, or some combination of these. In addition to a written dialogue of the interaction, the chaplain provides his reason for choosing this conversation, his interpretation of the encounter as an act of ministry to others, and how he would like his peers and supervisor to help. The script of the conversation is read aloud with members of the peer group assuming different roles, followed by a discussion.

The verbatim exercise conjures up insight into one's listening skills because it reveals: (1) what the chaplain recalls, (2) the parts of the conversation they decided were worth including in the dialogue, (3) what they believe they learned from the encounter, and (4) what peers notice that might have been missed by the chaplain. This final element can mercilessly expose listening "blind spots" of which the chaplain is completely unaware.

My stomach churns each time I consider the dialogue my colleague Mitch shared recounting his pastoral visit with the mother of a patient. After the peer group reading, our supervisor asked Mitch what at first glance appeared to be a rather innocuous question. "What do you take away from your interaction?" he asked.

"I think I am getting much better at listening," Mitch replied with a confident smile.

"Count the words."

"What?" asked Mitch.

"Count the words. More than half are yours. How well do you think you were listening?"

"I'm getting better . . . I think," said Mitch.

"You still have a long way to go. It seems your conversations are still more about you than those you are here to comfort and serve. Do you see that?" My heart ached for Mitch, but I knew our supervisor had zeroed in on his propensity to dominate every conversation—a trait that would limit his effectiveness as a chaplain.

The verbatim process also sensitized me to how a word can mean different things to different people. During one peer discussion, a colleague described how he had prayed for "a miracle" because that was what the family had requested. While the rest of us novice chaplains nodded in support, our supervisor found something worth exploring.

"Did you know what a miracle looked like for that family?" he asked. "Was it a cure? Was it an end to suffering? Could it have been something else?" We all sat in a stunned silence that seemed like an eternity until our supervisor bailed us out with this challenge: "It is your job as a chaplain to try to find out." It was reflective learning like this that made CPE so powerful and, at times, so personally painful.

Following my CPE experience, I developed a more acute awareness of when others were listening and when they didn't seem to be trying. I wondered what it would be like if we applied the verbatim-report practice to our daily conversations with family, friends, and even strangers. While having our own words replayed and assessed through the lens of others could expose how ineffective we are at practicing the art of listening, I suspect the resulting damage to relationships might not be worth the learning it offers.

In my interactions with Jacob, I was forced into the role of listener. During my CPE experience, the verbatim process pointed out major pitfalls to avoid when accepting that role. Together, these forays into poor practices revealed three duties required of anyone who wants to be effective in the listener role.

- *Listen with Your Presence:* In the third century BC, Greek philosopher Diogenes wrote, "We have two ears and one tongue so that we would listen more and talk less." This is much more than a biological truth. It offers timeless advice to consider being the listener as your default role in any conversation. Doing so demands setting aside all distractions and using body language and nonverbal cues to make the speaker feel he or she is the center of attention. Glancing at a watch suggests the desire to be somewhere else. A yawn implies boredom. Effective listening requires direct eye contact and resists interruption. Everything you do should reinforce that you are fully present for the speaker.

- *Listen with Curiosity:* The overarching goal here is to learn something new about the speaker. This requires approaching a discussion having no preconceived notions about where the conversation will lead. Open-ended comments like "What do you mean by that?" or "Tell me more about that" facilitate digging deeper while allowing the speaker to control the pace and direction of the talk. When approaching a conversation as a learning opportunity, the result can be like an excursion into uncharted territory where doors open to the wonder of unexpected scenery waiting to be discovered.

- *Listen with Your Heart:* This is the empathic side of listening, where the goal is to understand the emotions behind what has been said. It involves avoiding assumptions and asking what is meant by a word that is used. This may require practicing patience by honoring the speaker's silences. It may involve playing back what was said as a way of demonstrating they have been heard and understood. Restating comments confirms the listener has heard accurately and provides the speaker a chance to reflect on their own words.

***

My relationship with Jacob is better now because I approach our conversations with a different mindset. I accept that our relationship will always be one where my primary role is to be the listener. I am fine with that.

It occurs to me that few conversations can ever be equal opportunity talking sessions. Sometimes, I may have more on my mind that needs to be shared, while on other occasions, others may have more to say while I listen. While we don't need to go so far as counting words, we do need to be sensitive to who most needs to be heard in the moment.

Everyone you know has something on his or her mind, maybe trivial or perhaps troubling. Offering them the space to express it, to get it out in the open, is a powerful gift. This doesn't mean we need to solve a problem for them or offer sage advice. What is required is making them feel like they have been heard. Listening with your body, mind, and heart can help you get there.

---

[1] Edward Tufte, *Visual Explanations: Images and Quantities, Evidence and Narrative* (Cheshire, CT: Graphics Press, 1997).

Chapter Eleven

Friday-Morning Regulars

A restored 1950s MG convertible has the power to turn heads and bring in over thirty thousand dollars at an automobile auction. But the red one that pulled into a prime parking spot in front of Joey's Café did the unimaginable—brought all conversations inside to a halt.

Time stood still inside the easy diner. No sips of coffee, no bites of the specialty of the house, a pancake that draped over the edges of a large plate. The locals stared through the large picture window that spanned the southern wall to catch a view of the unexpected travelers from a distant place driving a vehicle from a different time.

I heard whispers all around me:

"Who are they?"

"Where are they going?"

"What kind of car is that?"

With the synchronized precision of a scene acted out many times before, attention returned to the center of each table the moment the couple entered the front door. The visitors moved toward a large table in the corner, only to be told by one resident that Mr. and Mrs. So-and-So usually sat there, forcing them to walk a gauntlet toward an open booth in the opposite corner of the dining area. The locals remained sequestered in their places, leaving only the waitress to talk to the strangers as she took their order. It was part of her job.

I knew how it felt to walk into this microcosm of the rural Midwest, having grown up a couple of miles outside this small town of Saint Anne, Illinois, until I left for college in 1971. Years later, the faces of the Joey's Café Friday-morning regulars were unfamiliar to me . . . and mine to them. They paused and stared when I entered too. Within a few seconds, I was welcomed because I arrived with their neighbors—my parents, who had lived there for over eighty years.

I wondered if these outsiders were reconsidering their decision to stop in this small village along the eastern Illinois backroads. Based on the view from my table, the couple seemed comfortable in their cameo roles at this local scene. Meanwhile, the townspeople effortlessly shifted back to chitchat about the latest local news, the new record price paid for area farmland, and the need for a good rain to nourish fields of corn, soybeans, and potatoes at their critical stage of summer growth.

I found the situation equal parts puzzling and troubling. The outward curiosity of the locals had evaporated when the couple had walked in the door. I wondered where it had gone. I pondered why no one had left their seat to greet the visitors. Did they not know what to say? Had they never experienced sitting *among* but not *in* the company of strangers? Feeling neither accepted nor shunned offers a kind of ambiguity that can be difficult to decipher.

I looked down at my plate for the next bite of breakfast sausage (patties, not links) and noticed the motto that was printed beneath the lacquered top of every table in Joey's Café. It read: "There are no strangers, only friends we haven't met yet." The gap between that promise and the current experience made the awkwardness of the situation even harder to bear. I felt compelled to extend a welcome, only to have a contrary thought fight back. I worried the locals might consider my attempt to welcome these visitors on their behalf a meddlesome overstep. I was receiving a refresher course on a simple truth I'd learned growing up here: the collective conscience of a small town is a powerful force.

I took one last sip of caffeine courage and walked the fifteen paces across the dining area to their table. "Hello. I grew up here but no longer live here," I said, a greeting designed to establish myself as an agent *for* the town but not a citizen *of* it. "I want to make sure you are feeling comfortable here."

"We're fine," replied the woman.

"We get it," added the man. "It's like *Cheers* for breakfast."

We engaged in casual conversation for a couple of minutes as they shared where they lived and their plans to attend an old car show a two-hour drive to the south. They asked about my connection with the community. It was a comfortable, easy talk.

When I returned to our table, I was bombarded with questions everybody wondered but would not seek answers for themselves:

"Who are they?"

"Where are they going?"

"What kind of car are they driving?"

I answered each one as best I could.

A half hour later, the couple took a final drink of coffee to wash down the slice of small-town indifference they had just been served. They paid their check and waved goodbye to the captive audience as they headed out the door. Speechless stares were offered in return. Outside the restaurant, our visitors climbed into their vintage vehicle and drove out of town. The normal chatter replaced the silence, perfectly bookending this alien encounter.

***

Those were good people, the Friday-morning regulars at Joey's, willing to do anything for their neighbors and friends. But even though the strangers looked like them in every imaginable way and never represented a threat, the townsfolk kept their distance. No one was impolite, but neither were they welcoming. When the visitors stood on the other side of the glass, no one could look away. When they were inside the restaurant, no one would meet their eye. Everyone was captivated by their arrival and departure but not their presence, raising a fundamental question for me: "How and where do we learn how to practice hospitality to others?"

To my knowledge, hospitality to others is a core tenet in all faith traditions. Most if not all the townspeople in Joey's that morning attended a Christian church each Sunday. Perhaps they forgot the advice found in Hebrews 13:2 that we should welcome strangers because they may be angels who have come to help us. If that's true, then for reasons of self-interest alone, we might want to accept the strangers in our midst.

We learn how to *practice hospitality* through experience, either as giver or receiver. For hospitality to happen, someone must take a risk. The couple who stopped at Joey's Café in the middle of their travels made the first move by entering an establishment full of people they did not know. Other than their stomachs being full, when they exited thirty minutes later, they left as they had arrived—as strangers.

Curiosity about the stranger—who they are, where they are headed—is a good place to start. Genuine hospitality demands that we translate a wary interest about others into caring and concern for them, because you never know who you might meet. To paraphrase the adage printed on each table at Joey's, everyone you know was a stranger before you met them—your best friend, your boss, your life partner, your favorite colleague.

Hospitality is a gift best served to strangers. Maybe we express it through a simple greeting, a smile, a wave goodbye—simple acts that signal a sense of welcoming. Isn't that how you would hope to be treated if you were one of the strangers in this story?

Chapter Twelve

Something More Precious

I wiped the tears away as I left his room that morning, a reflection of the combination of relief and regret I felt from knowing our sessions together would be coming to an end. Spending an hour with someone almost every week for over three years has a way of changing one's perspective—at least that was what my sessions with Richard did for me.

I'm not sure what I expected when I agreed to become a Stephen Minister, but when the church I attended was offering training, I signed up because it fit my desire to serve others, albeit in a less stressful context than the chaplain role (described in chapters ten and twenty-seven). A Stephen Minister develops a confidential, one-on-one caring relationship with an individual who is hurting while going through difficult life experiences. Richard fit that textbook description to a T.

Each Wednesday morning, I was given a front-row seat to one man's journey through some of the greatest challenges life can dish out. Richard was contending with his wife's Alzheimer's and the collateral damage that disease brings with it. He described how she'd stopped talking, stopped remembering his birthday and their anniversary, started slipping away. He cared for her the best he could while struggling through loneliness and his own health challenges. He changed his mind countless times as he wrestled with whether to remain in their home or move to a place where they could receive professional care. Inertia took over as competing sides of the ledger (one labeled "stay" and the other "go") grew longer each week.

In time, Richard realized he could no longer care for his wife on his own. Their move to an assisted living facility brought relief from caregiver responsibilities for him but accelerated his wife's decline. She stopped walking, stopped eating, and then one day stopped breathing. Richard's years of anticipatory grief did little to soften the blow. "We take so much for granted until we don't have it anymore," he said, choking through his tears.

My visits with Richard pulled me into an awareness of life events I had not experienced but feared await us all. Except for the couple of times I tightened his shoelaces (a self-care task his wife had performed for years due to his mobility issues), I felt helpless playing the role of "caregiver." I lacked the words to relieve his pain as he plowed the same emotional ground over and over again. I kept visiting Richard almost every week and did the only thing I knew how to do—listen.

Woody Allen is credited with saying "Eighty percent of life is showing up." Allen was speaking to aspiring writers when he shared the aphorism, one that has been repeated and reworded countless times. Allen advised that rather than spend energy worrying about when success might come their way, these novices should focus on writing their first play or novel instead. The product of their work would represent "showing up" for their profession.

I prefer to consider "showing up" though the lens of service to others. For people like Richard, the 80 percent figure understates the importance of "showing up" because, when someone is weighed down by life's heaviest burdens, knowing others are there for you can mean everything.

"Showing up" in service to others requires that we meet those in need where they are, both physically and emotionally. This is not as easy as it sounds because it runs counter to how we have been programmed to perform in school and at work, where rewards come from being prepared, speaking up, having answers, and achieving results. When "showing up" for others, a contrary set of principles apply. Being a caring presence for someone else requires honoring the silences, allowing them to control the conversation, helping them find answers for themselves, and expecting nothing in return. Practicing these principles may not seem like much, but allowing someone to feel they are the most important person in the world, if only for a few minutes, is a powerful gift.

This approach is in contrast with the "hero narrative" that permeates our culture. Expressed in literary tales of crisis and victory, the "hero narrative" promises things will change for the better when some preordained person with extraordinary power arrives on the scene and does something dramatic. It's an unfortunate myth because it takes the rest of us off the hook as we wait for the "hero" to appear. What we need instead is a contemporary "servant narrative" that recognizes the positive impact of "everyday heroes" who care for those in need. Helping others does not have to be recognized as "heroic" to be real. Authentic service is not about showing off; it is about showing up.

In her book *On Living*, hospice chaplain Kerry Egan described her discussions with a patient who constantly hounded nurses and doctors regarding the organ transplant he needed to survive but did not qualify for due to the severity of his condition. Egan wrote that her unique power as a chaplain came from the paradoxical fact that she made nothing transpire in the hospital. Unlike nurses, doctors, and social workers, she had no medications to give, no vital signs or signatures to take, and no programs and treatments to recommend to the patient. Her power lay in the simple act of showing up and listening. Egan suggested that because she had neither answers nor control, that problematic patient was eventually able to honestly share his fears and hopes.[1]

During the months following his wife's death, Richard's outlook gradually improved. He developed personal goals and habits to address his physical limitations. He sought ways to help others in the facility where he lived. He began moving forward on his own. "It's time for you to go help somebody who needs it more than I do," he said. I knew he was right.

As I stood to leave at the end of our final visit, Richard asked me to tighten his shoelaces. As I knelt in front of him, tears ran down his face as he said, "Since the first day you came to visit, I could talk to you without feeling judged. You listened. You've been a blessing to me."

"The blessing flows both ways," I replied as my tears matched his.

As I reflected on our time together, I realized how much I had gained spending time with Richard. He'd allowed me to witness the enormous resilience of the human spirit. Richard had shown me what it looked like to live out that "for better or for worse" phrase in one's wedding vows. He sensitized me to the fact that the decision my own ninety-plus-year-old parents faced regarding where to live was a complicated one that involved tradeoffs between safety and personal freedom. He showed me that everyday losses can be as devastating as the big ones. He offered compelling testimony to the power of holding tight to one's religious faith through the toughest of times. He reminded me not to take life for granted. Through memories and stories that expressed his love and loss, Richard revealed the beauty of a life well lived. More importantly, our relationship could no longer be defined using clinical terms like *caregiver* and *care-receiver*, because it had grown into something far more precious—we were now *friends*.

My visits with Richard made me realize that service to others begins when we *show up*. It can be the most meaningful thing we do because our very presence is the message.

---

[1] Kerry Egan, *On Living* (New York City: Riverhead Books, 2016), 66.

Chapter Thirteen

A Place to Grow

The dust was inescapable, tinting windows and clinging to every surface like a thin layer of paint. It was ginning season, and a mixture of cotton fiber, plant matter, and soil hung in the air like a fog too stubborn to lift. With only eighteen inches of annual rainfall here in the Texas Panhandle, Nature offered little remedy. "There's no shortage of dust here," I said to my friend Jim Newton as we approached the outskirts of his hometown of Brownfield. He shrugged in agreement at my understated depiction.

Jim was returning home with his childhood friend David Hahn more than forty years after they'd left Brownfield to pursue college and careers. David had taken flight after he obtained his pilot's license at the age of seventeen, while Jim had landed in a Dallas seminary before dedicating his life to serving others through music. Their high school buddies, JD and Danny, had returned to Brownfield after college graduation to raise families and follow careers in respected fields available in the local economy. JD had pursued education and was promoted to the prestigious position of superintendent of schools before retiring. Danny had leveraged his agricultural degree into a career with the Soil and Water Conservation District, established to promote sound farming practices in response to the devastating dust storms in the 1930s.

The four had kept in touch over the years, but they hoped these two days together would allow them to reconnect in more meaningful ways. It would turn out to be a reunion of contrasting life-journey scenarios: spreading one's wings and leaving familiar places and faces to pursue dreams away from home or sinking roots deeper in the community where one was raised.

The year was 2013, and I was along for the ride as part of a book project documenting the nonprofit organization Jim had founded thirty years earlier.[1] I was eager to witness how his childhood friends reacted to learning how far Jim had traveled from his Friday-night fame as star high school running back to bringing the healing power of music to severely ill children anywhere he could find them. I expected them to be impressed by the positive impact Jim had on the lives of thousands. Little did I realize at the time this would be a trip that would offer insight into my own uneasy relationship with the past that surfaced whenever I returned to my childhood home as an adult.

***

Brownfield, Texas, rests on the southern portion of the Central Great Plains that bisect the nation from north to south. Fifty miles to the east, outside the town of Post, the state road climbs westward more than one thousand feet to a windblown agricultural plateau as vast as it is flat. Geologists named this transition the Caprock Escarpment, the latter word the technical term for a steep slope that separates two level areas of different elevation. Locals simply call it the Caprock.

Like the opening scene from a *Beverly Hillbillies* episode, Model Ts packed with early settlers and all their earthly possessions found the climb a challenge. Since the gear ratio on the most popular vehicle of the twenties and thirties was lower in reverse, most turned their Fords around and backed up the incline. When they reached the top about an hour later, they caught their first glimpse of "heaven's tableland."

The flat topography offered a welcome change from the harsh landscape of buffalo grass, misshapen mesquite trees, and prickly pear cacti early settlers passed through to get there. I once heard someone describe that West Texas scrubland like this: "You can't call this *godforsaken country*, because if God had ever been there, he would never have left it that way."

The same cannot be said of the Caprock. For countless settlers, this agricultural "higher plain" offered hope for a future made possible by a resource invisible to the naked eye. The earliest farmers had no way of knowing their fields sat atop a large aquifer created during the most recent Ice Age. Stretching from South Dakota to the Texas Panhandle, the Ogallala Aquifer covers 174 thousand square miles, making it one of the largest in the world. It took local farmers years to discover it and learn how to be good stewards of this abundant but not endless life-giving resource located only a couple of hundred feet below the surface. Today, this underground lake still provides enough water to support the local agricultural economy despite the arid conditions.

Jim's and David's families arrived in Brownfield to pursue their versions of the American dream. For Jim's father, petroleum deposits discovered on the northern edge of the Permian Basin in the 1940s fueled his career in the oil business. David's family became cotton farmers, taking advantage of the inexpensive land to fulfill their dream of growing crops on property they owned instead of rented. Farmers like the Hahn family placed their faith in God but relied on the Ogallala Aquifer, a hidden resource possessing the power to sustain life.

***

A well-placed sign on the outskirts of town welcomed our arrival, boasting "Brownfield, Texas—A Place to Grow." At first blush, I found it a polite and welcoming message. But upon further consideration, the wording felt ambiguous, like something important had been omitted. Transitive verbs like *to grow* generate the expectation that a direct object might follow, but in this case, I was left to wonder whether Brownfield was a place "to grow crops" or "to grow a business" or something altogether different. Perhaps the local chamber of commerce had debated for hours but adjourned, unable to agree on how to complete the phrase. "Maybe I will find an answer during our two-day visit," I thought to myself.

It did not take long to discover little had changed since the four friends grew up here. After arriving at our motel, I asked Jim where I might buy a bottle of wine before settling in for the evening. "You'll have to travel forty miles north to Lubbock to find one," he chuckled. Terry County, where Brownfield was the county seat, remained "dry" in the legal sense of the word. Longstanding ordinances forbidding the sale of alcohol offered testament to the area's conservative Christian values and the power of the church to regulate moral standards through public policy.

The morning after we arrived, Jim, David, JD, and Danny rendezvoused at the former A&W Root Beer stand now named the Cub Café to capitalize on devotion to the high school team mascot. After a half hour of conversation over coffee and breakfast burritos, the four agreed a tour of their old stomping grounds was in order. They slipped into patterns of interaction established in their youth, as JD assumed the role of chauffeur and tour guide behind the wheel of his late-model Chevy Silverado dual-cab pickup. Jim grabbed the shotgun position while David, Danny, and I slid into the back seat with me in the middle. Except for my presence, it was easy to imagine the same pecking order of seat assignments four decades earlier.

JD suggested they start the tour by "making the drag," where, as teens, they would cruise at night until one driver ran short on gas, then switch to another vehicle to continue their hunt for a taste of local excitement. Rides up and down Route 82, Brownfield's primary north-south artery, became the center of their youthful universe, where they discovered a sense of freedom made possible by inexpensive gas and universal car ownership. Everyone laughed when Jim said, "Even at thirty-five cents a gallon, we spent a lot of money here."

They reminisced about girls kissed, pranks pulled, football games won and lost because of one great play or grand mistake. Familiar places evoked fond memories of friendly faces. Danny pointed out a small building on the edge of downtown that had once housed the office for the creators of Skip-Bo, a card game fashioned by JT and Skip Bowman. Passing by the high school, Jim mentioned an older student named Gary P. Nunn, whom they admired for his many talents. Nunn had made it big as a country music star in his home state and had been successful enough to tour with country music legend Jerry Jeff Walker's band. But he was best known as author of the song destined to become the unofficial anthem for the state of Texas: "London Homesick Blues."

Their tour demonstrated how change may not always represent progress. Care had failed to keep pace with the aging process for humble houses that were fresh and new fifty years ago. Well-known buildings were gone, leaving vacant lots and memories behind. Properties that remained were still referred to in relation to their past owners (as in, "That's the old Smith place"), reflecting a commonplace irony found in small towns where property becomes most strongly associated with a surname long after it has been sold to someone else.

JD's Silverado swung west out of town, past farmhouses and fields, before turning toward his house five miles to the south. The blacktop pavement was wide enough for two vehicles but lacked painted lines to define lanes, the county's way of granting implicit permission to drive down the middle of the road, which was exactly what JD was doing. David recounted a memory of seeing him drive his 1968 Oldsmobile 442 down this same stretch of road at more than 120 miles per hour when they were teens, all the encouragement JD needed to stomp on the accelerator. Within seconds, the speedometer climbed to 100 mph, limited to that speed only because someone had had the good judgment to place a governor on his engine.

With only his left hand on the wheel, JD twisted his upper torso to his right, a position that allowed him to make occasional eye contact with his audience in the rear seat while embellishing on his current story, paying closer attention to their reactions than either the low-tire-pressure indicator light illuminated on the dashboard or the narrow blacktop ahead. Hurtling down this country road, the four recaptured, at least for a few moments and miles, the thrill of excessive speed first discovered in their youth.

Despite the lively banter that surrounded me, I felt like I was descending into a circle of hell Dante could never have imagined. I was in control of nothing and saw danger everywhere I looked. I worried that some stray dog would make the ill-timed decision to cross the road in front of us. I imagined a tire blowout at any moment. I visualized the article in tomorrow's *Brownfield Gazette* reporting "Four former Brownfield High graduates killed in high-speed rollover crash south of town. Authorities still seeking information about the fifth passenger's identity and why he was with them." Since there was no escape, I offered up a silent prayer for safety.

Two hours later, our tour ended back at the Cub Café. Danny rushed inside to relieve himself, a predicament that explained his quietness during the latter part of the tour. JD apologized when he realized he had failed to provide the biological stop Danny had requested an hour earlier. I jumped out right behind Danny, thanking God that my feet were now planted on the firm ground of the parking lot.

As we stood outside, JD remarked how the colorful image painted on the side of Jim's Toyota resembled a tropical bird one might find on the front of a children's cereal box. (It was the logo for the nonprofit Jim founded.) I expected this would be the moment I had been waiting for, when these old friends moved their relationship from what they had done in the past to who they were today. I hoped JD and Danny would ask Jim about his career in service to thousands of severely ill children. But the inquiry stopped with JD's comment about the cartoonlike character on Jim's car door. Instead, we said our goodbyes and arranged for dinner together the next evening. I judged them severely in the moment for their lack of interest.

Jim had a different take. When I asked about his friends' lack of curiosity about his adult life serving others, he said, "That's not who I am to them."

***

There is a distinct difference between those who stay in their hometowns and those who leave. Those who remain tend to settle into known ways of thinking and acting, while those who move away are changed, often in unexpected ways. That was what I saw reflected in these two pairs of childhood friends. JD and Danny had found familiar careers close to where they had begun, while Jim and David had left town and found unexpected callings far from where they had been raised. Neither way is right or wrong, only different.

Perhaps this is a variant on the nature-versus-nurture debate. Is something intrinsic in those who move away that contributes to their propensity to change? Or do the experiences they encounter in new and unfamiliar worlds change them in ways those who stay behind never understand? I don't know.

But I do know that being a detached observer on this reunion trip exposed my bias toward the path of change, the one I had taken. It helped me come to grips with my own bittersweet visits back home, where I would look forward to leaving because I was placing too much value on the wrong definition of *recognize*. I had been looking for acknowledgment of how much I had changed—not a farm boy but a businessman, no longer a high school jock but a musician, not a child but a parent. By doing so, I'd missed the greater gift of still being regarded a part of their community, expressed through the unconditional acceptance they bestowed on me.

We each have people who, at some time in our lives, have mattered to us. They may be family, friends, teammates, or the larger community with which we once lived. If you decide not to follow Jim's example and rekindle old relationships, take a moment now and then to recognize that the shared experiences with those from your past remain an integral part of who you have become. By doing so, you can find a path toward *appreciating the ties that bind* us together in friendship with others.

***

As we reached the outskirts of Brownville on our trip back to Dallas, I glanced back at the same sign that had greeted us two days before. Taking part in the reunion of these childhood friends allowed me to complete its message. The easy way the four defaulted into habits and roles forged during their youth revealed how entangled their roots remained because they had been planted, side by side, on an agricultural plain in Brownfield, Texas: A Good Place to Grow Up.

---

[1] Larry V. Dykstra, *Music on a Mission: The Story of KidLinks* (Dallas: Inspired Forever Books, 2022).

Chapter Fourteen

Tale of Two Soldiers

The village hasn't changed much since I attended high school there more than forty years ago,

except for the Veterans Memorial that appeared in 2004 near the ball field on the edge of town.

Its installation was inspired by the death of Marine captain Ryan Beaupre, the first American

casualty of Operation Iraqi Freedom, killed when the helicopter he was copiloting crashed on

March 20, 2003.

Everyone in Saint Anne, Illinois, knew Ryan, which is the way it is in most towns with

only 1,200 residents. A popular child of the town, Ryan died on the first day of that conflict.

While the community responded by tying yellow and blue ribbons around trees, his death hit the

locals and our nation hard. Americans had expected a repeat of the Gulf War twelve years

earlier, when our nation had suffered few casualties. We were about to relearn the harsh truth

that wars don't work that way.

The memorial on South Second Avenue is dedicated to veterans of all American wars. Two

engraved markers flank the 105 mm Howitzer artillery cannon that is the centerpiece of the

display. The text on one marker begins: "All gave some, some gave all."

My father was one of those men who "gave some," although it took me decades to learn

that amount was far greater than I had realized. When I was a child, he shared a few stories about

his military service, but I now know these were the most pedestrian of tales. Like most proud

veterans described in Tom Brokaw's *The Greatest Generation*, Dad didn't feel the need to tell

others about his wartime experiences. He and his cohort accepted the moral demands of their

time, took on the enemy, returned home, and carried on. The real stories remained locked inside my father, out of sight but never out of mind. That is how most veterans handle their memories of war—with silence that is an extension of their call to serve their nation.

On Christmas Day of 1988, the gift of a world atlas opened Dad up to the idea of sharing more about his experiences. He was pointing to the map of Italy, where he had been stationed on this holiday forty-five years earlier, when my wife, Sandy, said, "You should write about your combat experiences." Early the next year, Dad began to capture that history. Aided only by a copy of his official flight record, he would sit in his living room and recall the people he had met and perils they had faced together during the war. Each evening my mother would type these handwritten memories on the IBM Selectric typewriter purchased for the project.

My brother, sister, and I were each given copies of their yearlong collaboration the next Christmas. The following day, I sat down to read his gift to us, expecting the story to begin in the days leading up to his enlistment. Instead, Dad grounded his story in a dream from his early childhood: "My desire was to become a baseball player."

I set down the manuscript as my heart sank at learning my father's personal wish, one that surprised me yet made perfect sense. The afternoons of hitting fly balls to his children, the countless hours he'd spent catching my throws as I'd practiced the art of pitching, his willingness to coach our summer softball team—these were all extensions of that dream. He had never told us that. Sadly, I had never thought to ask.

More than twenty-five years after receiving that initial draft of Dad's story, an idea tapped me on the shoulder and nudged me into action. Dad's 1988 memoir, or more likely the act of writing of it, had spurred him to revisit and reveal stories that before may have been too difficult to share. He sought out surviving members of his B-24 bomber crew, which led to multiple reunions. He located the sister of a fallen crewmate from Ottumwa, Iowa, and told her the story of his death. In return, she shared her brother's last letter home, in which he'd shared a premonition of his death the next day. Dad wrote multiple letters to the editor of the regional newspaper, the *Kankakee Daily Journal*. One published before Veteran's Day honored the ultimate sacrifices made by American soldiers, another during Black History Month acknowledged the excellent fighter support his squadron had received from the Tuskegee Airmen, and others defended the virtues of the B-24 aircraft that had carried him safely into and back from his missions over Eastern Europe.

My father shared details from events more than seventy years earlier that remained seared in his memory. His stories bore witness to bravery and cowardice, laughter and tears, tragedy and triumph. The fullness of his narrative was revealed bit by bit, and I found it compelling. I decided others needed to hear it, so I took on the task of incorporating the new information into his original manuscript. Six months later, Dad's story was published in the form of a book titled *In the Service of My Country: I Never Regretted a Day.*

In the concluding chapter, Dad summed up his story in this manner:

I have not written this memoir to set myself up as some sort of hero or glorify my service but to share a bit of American history before it is completely lost. It was worth every sacrifice I made to help free the world of such great oppression. I never regretted a day in the service of my country.[1]

I wasn't present to hand him the first copy of his book in June 2016, something I regret to this day. But Mom sent a picture of him seated in Joey's Café in Saint Anne, holding his book and smiling proudly for the camera.

Over the next few months my parents shared news about the extended family members and neighbors who had received a copy. Some readers knew little about the war or my father's service. One was moved to attempt to get Dad awarded the Purple Heart medal he had refused seventy years earlier because he knew two of his crewmates would receive the award posthumously, which, in his mind, made the shrapnel wound in his leg trivial in comparison. Another reader started addressing him as "my hero." A teacher from Saint Anne Elementary School gave her students copies of the book for their Veteran's Day reading assignment and invited him to speak to the class. The positive impact that Dad's story was having on others had progressed far beyond my modest expectations.

A few months later, I traveled to Illinois to see my parents. Naturally, a visit to Joey's Café was on our itinerary since this remained a vital part of my parents' weekly routine. We had finished breakfast and were headed toward the door when a gentleman signaled me to his table. I wasn't sure who he was, but the invitation was too unmistakable to ignore, so I walked over to him. "I just wanted to tell you how nice a job you did with your dad's book," he said.

"Thanks," I replied. "I just wanted to give Dad the gift of his story while he is still here and can appreciate it."

"You gave a gift to the entire village," he said. His comment stuck with me for days.

Initially, I accepted his remark as a positive book review from another detached reader. I learned later the gentleman was Mark Beaupre, father of Ryan. Mark had shared his son's war story with the press and the community, including a letter Ryan had written to his family, forwarded by a friend who had agreed to send it in the event of his death. In that letter, Ryan had written:

It was my choice to go into the military. . . . Realize that I died doing something that I truly love, and for a purpose greater than myself.

Mark's comment to me about the larger impact of my dad's book, and his openness to share his son's final letter, demonstrated the power our stories possess to bring us together in our common humanity. I suspect that my dad's story resonated with Mark because he knew firsthand the most painful loss our wars dish out. Just as surely, Mark's sharing of Ryan's final letter provided understanding and comfort to people he will never meet.

Sharing our stories allows us to affirm who we are and appreciate the commonalities between ourselves and others. The war experiences of Capt. Ryan Beaupre and Sgt. Ralph Dykstra were separated by nearly sixty years, yet both proudly served their country. Together, they complete and reframe the quote engraved on a small memorial on the edge of Saint Anne, Illinois: "Ryan gave all, Ralph gave much."[2] Both, through their stories, remind us what it means to be a hero. Despite their sacrifices, neither regretted a day in the service of their country.

We each have a story to tell. We may not realize it, but there may be something from our lives that others will find to be a gift in ways we can never imagine. Likewise, we can be enriched through hearing the stories others have to share with us. It is imperative that you *share your story* and seek out the stories of those around you.

---

[1] Ralph Dykstra, *In the Service of My Country: I Never Regretted a Day*, ed. Larry V. Dykstra (Dallas: Inspired Forever Books, 2016), 127.

[2] I shared this chapter with my father's friend, Vietnam War veteran Rodney Franklin. He commented that even those who "gave much" also "gave all" during their time in the service of their country. While I did not revise this line of text, I trust that Rodney's observation is accurate and worthy of note.

Chapter Fifteen

A Fish Story

Childhood memories flooded back when I learned that my Uncle Kenny had passed away after ninety-three vibrant years on this earth. Every time someone connected to me dies, I think about them in a more deliberate and focused manner, reflecting on the virtues and values they demonstrated while here with us.

Before the age of ten, I spent more time with Uncle Kenny and Aunt Lois than most of my other relatives. Many summers, my siblings and I were shipped off to their home in Ottawa, Illinois, where we would stay with our cousins and become part of their family for a week. Uncle Kenny's confident persona balanced with Aunt Lois's joyful spirit made them a team adept at converting daily life into experiences worth remembering.

During our stays with them, we pursued activities unavailable at home on the farm. When I was six years old, Uncle Kenny convinced a river barge pilot to let us kids ride his pusher craft twenty miles downstream, where Uncle Kenny would pick us up. It was my first boat trip, and the opening and closing of gates and the changing water levels as we passed through a lock and dam boggled my childhood mind. On another visit, when Uncle Kenny and Aunt Lois took us hiking in nearby Starved Rock State Park, he told us about the three suburban Chicago women who had gone on a similar excursion earlier that spring and never returned. Their bodies had been found in a nearby cave. I don't believe he shared that information to scare us that day but to transform our simple walk in the park into a memory. Uncle Kenny knew the recipe for any memorable experience required a dash of perceived adventure.

The highlight of our weeks in Ottawa were the trips to the grain elevator Uncle Kenny managed outside of town on the banks of the Illinois River. One day he took us to the top of his grain silo, 120 feet above the ground. It was the first time I'd experienced the feeling I get every time I stand on anything higher than a step stool—a tingling in my pelvic region like some force is grabbing my private parts to make sure I am paying attention. That distressing sensation was repaid by the panoramic view of the wide river meandering westward across the expansive prairie unlike anything this seven-year-old had ever seen.

The black-and-white television mounted in Uncle Kenny's dusty office was always set on WGN-TV, the Chicago station that broadcast Cubs baseball games (always played in daytime before lights were added to Wrigley Field in 1988). I found it curious that Uncle Kenny turned the TV volume off, replacing it with radio play-by-play on sister station WGN-AM. Uncle Kenny knew enough about baseball from his years of playing in high school and college to realize a more insightful depiction of the game would be offered by Jack Quinlan and Lou Boudreau than by TV announcer Jack Brickhouse. While Brickhouse was eventually admitted into the American Sportscasters Association Hall of Fame, he relied on the new medium of the television screen to tell the story, supplementing it with his colorless "Ball one . . . ball two . . . strike one" voice-over. I suspect that Uncle Kenny avoided his parse play-by-play reporting because he believed life demanded more than allowing action to speak for itself. Amplifying each situation to the greatest degree was Uncle Kenny's way of proclaiming the richness of life.

My fondest memory of our summer visits was the day Aunt Lois took us fishing along the river near the grain silo. After unloading a bundle of bamboo poles and a pail of bait from the car, she positioned us children along a small landing a couple hundred yards from Uncle Kenny's office. She slid a night crawler on the hook and cast the line into the water. I knew nothing about fishing and possessed even less interest in the activity, but Aunt Lois's youthful exuberance was not to be denied. Framed beneath her carrot-red hair, a broad smile lit up her face as she placed the pole in my hand. In a unique voice that blended laughter and speech, Aunt Lois said, "Here you go, Larry. Catch something."

I stood frozen with rod in hand as my aunt moved to assist the other novices in our fishing party. The line lay motionless, floating on the surface, which I figured didn't matter because I doubted there were any fish inhabiting the muddy water below. A couple of minutes later the fishing gods showered their blessing my way. The line surged, and the pole came alive with an unexpected energy that pulled me a step or two closer to the water's edge, where I held on tight.

"You've got one!" cried Aunt Lois.

I imagine the look on my face reflected more confusion than excitement, because our angling training had not covered what to do in the event a fish took the bait. Sensing my need for help, Aunt Lois grabbed the pole from my hand and reeled in our bountiful catch: a foot-long carp. Once we had it onshore, she handed me the line with a wiggling creature dangling below. She directed me to hold it high in the air so she could take a photograph documenting our prize capture of the day.

Over the next few days, I lived out the meaning of the term *fish story*. Uncle Kenny and Aunt Lois made me the hero of the fable, telling everyone how "Larry caught a huge fish . . . one over a foot long. . . . It was amazing!" Despite their claims, the voice of my conscience recognized that this was exaggeration that bordered on outright lie. In my mind, the facts were undeniable: I didn't bring the equipment or the bait. I was afraid to touch a slimy worm, much less place it on the hook. I didn't cast the line into the river. I didn't reel that bottom-feeder out of the water toward its demise. My sole contribution had been, by chance alone, to be the person holding the pole when the carp had a craving for a midday snack. Deep inside, I knew the truth: *I did not catch that fish!* My parents would have been proud of the fact that even at the innocent age of eight, I understood I should never take credit for something I did not do.

Today I see this fish story in a different light. What I interpreted as undeserved credit for an achievement was an expression of unconditional affirmation that defined the character of both my beloved uncle and aunt. Making this *my* catch was an example of the kind of gifts they showered on others throughout their lives. Uncle Kenny and Aunt Lois understood their duty to build others up, tell them they mattered, and make them feel special whether they deserved it or not.

The words we share with those around us have a profound impact. Pointing out the negatives of any person or situation is easy. However, love is expressed when we look for the strengths of others and use our words intentionally to recognize, encourage, and inspire. I know my cousins understand this truth because they expressed it so clearly in their father's obituary:

> *Kenneth Ralph Ahrens, 93 years young, known as Poppy to those who loved him the most, was called home to heaven on Friday, January 5th. . . . He taught us to live life to the fullest, always give it our best, and be kind to others. In lieu of sending flowers, the family invites you to honor Poppy's life by taking a walk in the sunshine, sharing a joke with a friend, or making a hole-in-one!*

The sun is shining outside my home today, so I think I will go for a long walk and let its warmth touch my face, nourish my memories of Uncle Kenny and Aunt Lois, and brighten my soul. I pray that feeling will grow into an enduring reminder of my duty to affirm the goodness that resides in others, because in doing so we profess the goodness in us all.

Maybe that will require reshaping the truth a bit, like telling someone they look better than they might or that they are better at something than they may believe themselves to be. And if I really buy into this code of affirmation, maybe I'll find a way to congratulate someone on the fish they caught all by themselves, even though they just happened to be holding the pole when an unfortunate fish got a case of the munchies. That's what my Uncle Kenny and Aunt Lois did for me. That's what I need to do . . . *affirm others*.

Chapter Sixteen

The Wisdom of the Bus

Sandy is a far more comfortable traveler than me. Journeying into unknown lands and cultures elicits my wife's adventurous spirit. Positive energy flourishes with her eagerness to discover what new experiences may await around the corner. It impresses me every time I see it.

But no matter how hard I try to will that quality into myself when we travel, I fall short. While Sandy is looking forward to getting to know the next person she meets, I may be analyzing the present situation and assessing any and all risks, no matter how small their probability. Given these contrasting orientations, it is surprising we travel together as well as we do. Our differences complement each other, except in those moments when, well, they don't.

Gender differences reinforce different mindsets toward adventure and travel. In an enduring stereotype grounded in truth, dudes like me don't like to ask for directions when they get "lost." Guys tend to be so averse to revealing any sign they are not in complete control they might not even speak the "L-word." Women, on the other hand, seem to have no problem admitting this reality when it happens. Sandy treats being lost as an opportunity to open a conversation with someone who might become a new friend. It's like the two genders are looking at the same animal from opposite ends of a telescope: one spots a large tiger ready to pounce, while the other sees a small approachable kitten.

I try to imagine an anthropological explanation for this difference. Perhaps while cavemen were stealthily stalking prey for that night's dinner, their wives were simply asking the women in the next village where the nearest grocery store was located. Your theory is as good as mine.

Nonetheless, it is no mystery why it takes thousands of male sperm to fertilize a single female egg; men refuse to ask for directions.

During a recent vacation together, Sandy and I decided to visit an attraction on the other side of Mérida, Mexico, a provincial town in the center of the Yucatán Peninsula. Neither of us knew how to get there, but Sandy advocated taking public transportation. In her mind, the bus represented the more adventuresome and frugal option. In mine, that option carried a higher probability of something going awry.

On this occasion, we went with her preference. But shortly after we boarded the local bus and were on our way, my internal compass started poking me in the ribs, telling me we were headed the wrong direction. This was a concern Sandy did not share, leaving me boxed into the classic male mind trap: I doubted we were going the right way, but at the same time, I was too stubborn to ask anyone if that was the case.

Sensing my anxiety with our situation (she'd seen this a few times before), Sandy honored my need for certainty from a reliable source. Naturally, the task of asking for directions would fall on her due to her superior mastery of the Spanish language. (Honestly, language was not the reason the duty fell to her. I probably wouldn't have asked for directions even if everyone on the bus spoke English.) Sandy didn't jump right into action like I hoped she would. She scanned the bus for the right subject to approach instead. This plan of attack produced a delay that required me to stew in my destination anxiety a bit longer.

When she finally sprang into action, her first move seemed like the logical choice to me. She questioned our bus driver, who confirmed that we had chosen the right bus, an answer that satisfied me. After all, he was employed in the transportation industry and, perhaps more on point, was male (and men never get lost).

But then, to my surprise, Sandy turned to two local women seated together in a front row and asked them for their perspective regarding the correctness of our route. Within a few moments, a couple of other riders seated nearby joined in what by now had evolved into an animated discussion. My rudimentary understanding of Spanish told me they were talking about much more than destination coordinates. The locals were offering suggestions about what we might want to see while we were visiting their town. Relationships had somehow transitioned from strangers traveling on the same urban bus into an impromptu hospitality group.

As I watched her interact with the locals, I became impressed with how much fun Sandy was having. I watched as her vibrant persona began to shine more brightly as she chatted and laughed with people who moments earlier had been complete strangers. She had invited herself into their world with her request for help, and they had welcomed her as a guest in their city with their responses. By getting to know them as real people, Sandy was learning about much more than bus routes. She was showing me (again) how a situation I found stressful could be converted into one where people come together and experience their common humanity.

Finally, the moment arrived when her conversation with her new friends reached a lull. I sidled up to her and asked, "Why are you still asking all of these people for directions?"

"It's quite simple," she replied. "The more people who know where you want to go, the more support you have, and the more likely you are to get there."

I let that sink in for the next few minutes, days, weeks . . .

***

Sandy's approach to asking for directions is instructive regarding how to navigate the uncharted waters of our lives and careers. Certainly, these journeys are more complex than confirming you are on the right bus in an unfamiliar city. Just like our fellow commuters in that Mérida city bus, there is wisdom all around that can be of great help, just for the asking. It is not a stretch to suggest that success may be found by following these "wisdom of the bus" principles: tell others from diverse perspectives where you want to go, share your uncertainty about the path you are traveling, and invite them to help navigate you toward your destination. As Sandy said, "The more people who know where you want to go . . . the more likely you are to get there."

Summary of Part II

Lessons I Have Learned from my Relationships with Others

- Let empathy be your teacher. Find ways to understand what others are going through and feeling.

- Listen to learn. Everyone you know has something on their mind. Listening with your body, mind, and heart is a powerful gift.

- Practice hospitality. Be welcoming to guests. Everyone you know was a stranger before you met them.

- Show up for others. Your very presence sends an unmistakable message of caring.

- Appreciate the ties that bind. We each have people who matter to us. Take a moment now and then to hold them in your memory and keep them in your heart.

- Share your story. There may be something from our lives that others will find helpful in ways you could never imagine.

- Affirm others. When we recognize the goodness that resides in others, we profess the goodness in us all.

- Ask for help. The more people who know where you want to go, the more likely you are to get there.

Part III: World

Using the word *world* to describe this section might lead you readers to expect stories about my high adventures trotting the globe, during which I learned about exotic people and places, the unusual customs and cuisines of distant lands. That is not what awaits in the pages ahead. Nor will I be sharing reflections from an extended visit to Walden Pond, where I gained a deeper connection with Nature. Neither of these views of *world* will be offered here.

No single definition fits what I have in mind to capture the overarching theme for the next eight stories. Allow me to offer this personalized combination of definitions: a *world* is where "a social creature" becomes involved in some "sphere, realm, or domain" related to "human endeavors." While I am certain even a church committee could have arrived at language that doesn't feel like such a mangled and meaningless compromise, this description fits what I have in mind, and I'm sticking with it.

Be forewarned. The chapters ahead look and sound nothing like a third-party travelogue. Instead, expect stories that take place in familiar, maybe even mundane, settings. What distinguishes them is how each was incited by a situation that pierced my consciousness and pointed me toward a noteworthy insight or principle. These are stories that showed me, sometimes in very unexpected ways, how to navigate through this world and get more out of life. They reveal principles to apply going forward such as slowing down, taking notice, defining success, and exploring nearby "worlds" already accessible to us.

Chapter Seventeen

Under the Table

"That must have taken a big dent out of somebody's budget," I thought to myself when I saw it the first time. Measuring over fifteen feet long and six feet wide, the table curved its way inside the Product Development Conference Room like a racetrack. Its gray Formica top was inlaid with our corporate logo at regular three-foot intervals around the perimeter. Once I had sat at that table a few times, I couldn't help but feel it was worth every penny, a fitting tribute to our multibillion-dollar pizza brand.

It was around the year 2000, and we had been on a roll at Pizza Hut following a series of new product successes such as Stuffed Crust Pizza, the Big New Yorker, and the P'Zone, to name only a few. You can visualize our product development process like a funnel with numerous ideas going in but only a few flowing into the marketplace. Each potential innovation faced numerous hurdles along the way, a key one being the regular updates on the status of our new product pipeline to senior management around this table. This conference room was the place where the futures of countless new product innovations and a few careers would be considered and judged. Many of the ideas served from this table would be launched nationally and become household names. More became pizza flotsam, failing to navigate the multiple gates in the new product go-to-market gauntlet.

I am certain some of the best pizzas ever served were eaten in this space, each one hot and fresh, right out of the test-kitchen ovens, prepared by pizza masters whose job descriptions included training thousands of hourly employees to execute their product designs. I have heard it said, "There is no such thing as a bad pizza." While experience has taught me the folly in this statement, it was an accurate description of every pie served here.

Not all was perfect with this stage where the best pizzas imaginable were showcased. Our beautiful, branded table possessed an audible flaw. Well out of sight but rarely out of ear, it chirped like a solitary cricket every time someone leaned into, onto, or away from it. I am not sure when it first started, but the creak became a regular "speaker" at our meetings.

The squeak bothered us all at first, like a team member who didn't know when to stop talking. We would complain to each other about the annoyance before moving on to the more pressing agenda items. With time, our irritation with its song faded into the background. In the lexicon of our corporate culture at the time, the noise became a "gravity issue"—something we could do nothing about and, therefore, needed to accept and move forward from.

One remarkable trait of human beings is our ability to adapt to our surroundings, including acclimating to aspects of our environment that bother us. Such was the case with our talking table. Our thinking followed a predictable pattern of moving from "We should do something about this" to "Someone should do something about this" to something we no longer mentioned. In time, our complaints fell into silent acceptance.

I don't recall what triggered it, but one day I noticed the irksome chirp as if for the first time. Maybe I was not as engaged as I should have been in the discussion, or maybe someone leaned against the table with greater force than usual. But there it was again in my consciousness, emanating from all areas beneath its surface, louder and more menacing than before. I imagined our solitary cricket had been joined by a choir of talkative pests now singing in unison.

The harder I tried to block out the sound, the louder it rang in my ears, mocking my very intent. I found myself channeling an unnamed narrator from a Poe short story as the "telltale cricket's" volume grew louder inside my head with each chirp. "I must do something about this!" I resolved.

When the meeting concluded and everyone had left the room, I crawled under the table to diagnose the source of the squeak. My private reconnaissance mission revealed that even the slightest movement of the immense top caused it to rub against either of the two large vertical cylinders that supported it. Finding a way to prevent that movement would stop the shifting and, by extension, the noise. The problem defined, I launched a plan of attack to rid us once and for all from this aural annoyance.

The following Saturday I made a visit to the conference room carrying the tools of my newly adopted noise-abatement trade. With a hammer and a dozen shims in hand, I crawled under the table and began driving the tapered pieces of wood where the underside of the table and the supporting cylinders met. At first, the space between these parts was large enough for the shims to be driven in their entire length. But with each additional shim, the gaps grew smaller until, after about five or six were in place between the tabletop and both pillars beneath, the structure became stable. When I tested my work by leaning onto it from above with both elbows, there was not a sound to be heard. Never had silence sounded so beautiful!

A couple of days later, I attended my first meeting in the conference room, eager to learn if my repair held up and whether my peers would notice the genius of my handiwork. The answers to these questions were *yes* and *no*, in that order. I was delighted that the bothersome squeak had been muted, but the table's newfound silence took on the cloak of secrecy. No one noticed. So, like the table, I endured the meeting in silence, hoping that some form of recognition for my initiative might arrive. It never did.

Upon reflection, the lack of credit was an inevitable outcome given my approach. I had made this *my* initiative, and all my actions demonstrated that intent. I went to the room to scout the problem when no one else was present. I made repairs on a weekend when others were unlikely to be there. I never spoke of my plans to any of my colleagues. My plot for the story cast myself as the hero.

Our squeaky table had offered an opportunity for collaborative problem-solving that I had missed. Irritation with the noise was a group problem that had invited a shared solution, both in terms of developing a plan and executing it. Instead of using the challenge as an opportunity to build camaraderie among a team, I had chosen to go it alone and demonstrate my initiative and ability to right the wrong.

According to reliable sources, the table is gone now, victim of an updated corporate logo and the company's move to a new office building.

***

Today, I consider this tale of the table a metaphor for a corporate version of *bystander apathy*—a social psychology phenomenon where individuals are less likely to take action when others who are present could. When no one does anything, the situation gets interpreted as not being important enough to merit action. In this vicious cycle, responsibility is diffused (shoved under the table, if you will) and left for someone else to deal with later.

There are problems all around that are far more serious than a table that emits a high-pitched chirp matching that of a cricket. One lesson here is that the squeak emanating from beneath was part of the table's essence, a little quirk that lent it personality while reminding us that nothing is perfect. But this story also teaches that the sources of our irritation won't go away because of our complaining, that there is no point in raising issues unless we are willing to do something about them. While my solo approach may have been flawed, I believe my extermination effort points to an important principle for us all: If something is not working or is annoying, *take initiative* and fix it!

Opportunities for improvement present themselves in all shapes and sizes. Perhaps it's an issue with the format of a data report, a consumer complaint that begs for a solution, or a leaky bathroom faucet at home. Whatever the situation, if we put as much energy into solving problems as we do into identifying and complaining about them, the world around us will be a much better place.

Chapter Eighteen

The Piece I Missed

I love *tortilla espanola*. Despite its simplicity, or perhaps because of it, I can't get enough of this staple akin to a potato omelet each time I travel to Spain. I discovered that *tortilla espanola*, in addition to being a great tapa, worked as a good source of carbohydrates during late-morning breaks on my long treks on the Camino de Santiago.

After starting together in Pamplona, Sandy and I walked in good company on the Camino for the first twenty-one days. Poor tactical planning on our part, leaving a bag with valuables checked in a Madrid train station, necessitated her to leave the Camino to retrieve it. This gave her the chance to catch up with Spanish friends while allowing me to experience the pilgrimage route on my own. Eight days later, I arrived in the expansive cobblestone plaza outside the cathedral in Santiago de Compostela, and Sandy was there to meet me.

During my week walking solo on the Camino, I met two pilgrims who had both been on the Camino far longer than me. Nina was a middle-aged woman who had left her home in Geneva three months earlier, while Irishman Michael had been walking for six months. As we chatted over dinner on consecutive nights, each shared a desire to slow down and savor their last few days on the Camino. I had been pushing myself through longer days of walking so I could reach Santiago on the same day Sandy planned to arrive there. Given the perspectives of these fellow travelers, I wondered if my case of "get-there-itis" was causing me to miss out on something.

A couple of days later, I was passing through one of the small farm villages that dot the Spanish landscape. The town had no café bars offering food or drink, so I set my mind on continuing to the next village. As I neared the last house on the edge of town, an older gentleman crossed the road a few feet ahead of me, trailed by a parade of a dozen chickens. A moment later, an elderly woman who I assumed was his wife appeared from around the corner holding a plate of *tortilla espanola*. Standing face to face with me, she extended her arms and said, "Caliente," an indication the dish had just left her stovetop. Without hesitating, I replied "No, gracias" and kept walking.

That scene haunted me for miles, for weeks, and then for months. Certainly, I missed out on a tasty treat, but I also missed a chance to receive one woman's generosity. Maybe my acceptance of that small act of kindness would have been a needed blessing to her. Why didn't I stop and allow her to experience the joy that comes from offering a gift to others? Refusing to accept that woman's gesture of hospitality was my deepest regret from my twenty-nine days walking the Camino.

Declining her offer made me wonder if I possessed some flaw that kept me from slowing down. Sandy had reminded me on many occasions that life is a journey, not a destination, but that advice didn't always translate into spontaneity on my part. It certainly didn't in the case of the offer I declined in that small Spanish village.

***

A few years later, I read about the experiment conducted by the *Washington Post*[1] that assured me that I was not alone when it comes to my inability to slow down and accept gifts offered free for the taking. Editors at the *Post* convinced one of the world's greatest violinists, Joshua Bell, to stand in a Washington, DC, subway station during morning rush hour and perform six classical masterpieces. They wanted to learn if placing the performer and his music out of context—in a busy metro stop instead of a grand concert hall—would prevent passersby from pausing to appreciate Bell's immense talent.

As they prepared for the event, *Post* staff worried that crowd-control problems might arise when commuters clogged the station once they recognized Bell and stopped to listen. Their concerns were unfounded. While Bell played for forty-three minutes on a Stradivarius violin valued at over three million dollars, 1,097 people walked past him. Twenty-seven commuters dropped tips totaling $32.17 in his violin case. Only seven people (about half of 1 percent) stopped for at least one minute to listen to the virtuoso.

The *Washington Post* experiment was conceived of as a study of the power of context. However, the results raised a more fundamental question regarding what we might be failing to notice as we sleepwalk through our daily lives.-My bet is we are missing a lot.

Learning to slow down and appreciate the world in which you live requires conscious effort. While practicing mindfulness might be a good place to start, shaking up some of your well-seeded patterns of behavior might work as well. You don't need to sign up for a training program to begin slowing down. As you approach any daily activity, think about what you would normally do, and then do something completely different. Maybe that's taking a different route home from work, putting your watch on the other wrist, or eating your dessert before the entrée. You decide. Then consider these questions: What do you notice? What surprises you? How does it feel? Did you observe anything new about familiar people, places, activities, and objects that occupy your world?

Slowing down doesn't mean becoming less productive. Even if it makes you feel like you are missing out on the rapid pace of the rat race, chances are you will be gaining more in return. Traveling through life at a more deliberate pace allows us to think more clearly about the challenges we face, consider and weigh more options, and make better decisions as a result. Better yet, our ability to appreciate the world that surrounds us will improve, as will our capacity to be present with others and experience relationships with them in a deeper way. Slowing down may even prevent you from missing out on something unexpected, such as an invitation from a stranger to sample a piece of *tortilla espanola*.

A lifetime consists of a series of brief moments, so making each one matter will make our lives matter more as a result.

---

[1] Gene Weingarten, "Pearls Before Breakfast: Can one of the nation's great musicians cut through the fog of a D.C. rush hour? Let's find out," *Washington Post*, April 7, 2007, https://www.washingtonpost.com/lifestyle/magazine/pearls-before-breakfast-can-one-of-the-nations-great-musicians-cut-through-the-fog-of-a-dc-rush-hour-lets-find-out/2014/09/23/8a6d46da-4331-11e4-b47c-f5889e061e5f_story.html.

Chapter Nineteen

The Persuasive Edge

The image on my parents' black-and-white television grabbed our attention in a way most commercials do not. A man resembling a twentysomething version of magician David Copperfield sat holding a microphone beneath his chin. Standing beside him, an announcer dressed in a business suit introduced the action in a resonant voice reminiscent of the beloved anchorman from the 1960s and '70s, Walter Cronkite:

"With an ordinary credit card, we're going to prove that Edge lets you shave closer than the leading foam. First, listen to an unshaven face."

The reporter swiped the card along the right cheek: *Scrape, scrape.* Then he repeated the move across the left cheek: *Scrape, scrape.*

"Now, we'll shave the left side with foam, the right side with Edge."

As the subject pulled the razor across his face, the reporter said, "Edge lubricates as it lathers, so we can press harder to shave closer than foam."

As the phrase "Thirty Minutes Later" was superimposed over the screen, our reporter continued: "Now, listen to the foam side." *SCRAPE, SCRAPE.* "Then listen to the Edge side." *Scrape, scrape.* "Foam." *SCRAPE.* "Edge." *Scrape.* "Edge lets you shave closer than the leading foam."

A flurry of responses by my brother, Curt; brother-in-law, Don; and me expressed our collective doubt.

"That can't be true!"

"I bet the test was rigged."

"What's a shaving gel?"

I was a senior in high school at the time and possessed at least five fewer years of shaving experience than the two of them, so I respected their superior whisker wisdom. As chance would have it, Don possessed a credit card and a can of Foamy, while Curt somehow had purchased a can of Edge Shaving Gel. "Let's give it a try!" we agreed.

Our game plan kicked off with Curt sneaking away to shave in private. When he returned, Don swiped his credit card upward across each side of his face. The difference was subtle yet audible. One side: *SCRAPE, SCRAPE.* The other side: *Scrape, scrape.* Curt confirmed what our ears told us. Foam side: *SCRAPE.* Edge side: *Scrape.*

Our reenactment made a lasting impression on me, so much so that I have remained a loyal Edge user to this day. I attribute my devotion to the way its blue gel transforms into a white lather when I rub it over my face, converting shaving from a mundane chore into a magical experience. But I must admit the functional benefit portrayed in the original commercial no doubt served as a catalyst for my initial trial of the product.

Product-demonstration ads intended to show that a product is superior to competition have been popular for decades and are still used today. The effectiveness of this approach depends on execution. The marketing team at Edge Shaving Gel enjoyed an unforeseen advantage: Their commercial was the work of future filmmaker John Hughes, who would later write, produce, and direct some of the most successful coming-of-age comedy movies of the 1980s and 1990s.[1] In this ad for a new shaving product, Hughes applied one of the axioms of great storytelling: "Show, don't tell." Even though Hughes didn't completely convince the three of us, his ad moved us toward self-discovery, where something more powerful happened—we persuaded ourselves.

***

It took me years to apply this "show, don't tell" principle to my work as leader of consumer insights for the nation's largest pizza chain. A researcher by training and orientation, I was well suited for a career that required me to analyze and present information to guide decision-makers. One platform for achieving this goal at Pizza Hut was a quarterly presentation titled "The Voice of the Consumer," which integrated data from different sources to reveal our brand strengths, weaknesses, and opportunities relative to competition. This external perspective was intended to balance the wants and needs of consumers who purchased our products with internal priorities advanced by functional leaders, such as operational efficiency and profitability.

One business issue to emerge from my analyses was the difficulties customers encountered during the front end of the pizza-ordering process. In an era before online ordering, about two-thirds of all pizza transactions began with a telephone call. Based on consumer feedback, our restaurants were less effective at answering the phones and more likely to place customers on hold compared to our competitors. While I believed this evidence was convincing enough to dedicate resources toward improving this weakness, most members of our management team were not swayed. One executive expressed doubt by saying, "If someone gets a busy signal, they'll just wait a few minutes and call us back." Since most pizza-delivery orders begin when a group of people are already hungry, I believed they would call a different pizza place, but I lacked indisputable evidence to support my view or challenge his. Despite multiple presentations highlighting this operational weakness, I was unable to convince management of the need to take action.

A serendipitous request from our president to introduce his senior team to the next generation of pizza eaters (whom we today call millennials) paved the way toward acceptance.

The population growth represented by children of baby boomers combined with historically high pizza-consumption rates among teenagers meant the long-term success of our business demanded we make our brand relevant to this demographic segment. To sensitize his senior team to the beliefs and behaviors of the millennials, our president asked me to organize an event where they could interact with and better understand this generational cohort.

A few months later, nine members of our executive team greeted an equal number of adolescents at a hotel conference room in Austin, Texas. After taking our seats around a large table, we took turns introducing ourselves before moving to an open-ended discussion. We asked these youths to share what was going on in their lives, where they received their information about new products, the restaurants they visited, and their likes and dislikes regarding pizza.

Following an hour-long discussion, I suggested our guests break into teams and order pizzas from the three largest national chains. Three adolescent women were invited to order from one of our competitors, a mixed-gender group from a different pizza chain, and three young men from our brand. The first two teams completed their orders routinely, but when one of the young gentlemen (let's call him Randy) called one of our restaurants, the trouble began. His call was answered after a couple of rings, but the conversation stumbled and stalled as our caller encountered obstacles at each step of the ordering process. Randy would place his hand over his phone during the long silences to provide us with updates. "It's her first day on the job. . . . She hasn't been trained. . . . She doesn't know how to enter an order on the computer. . . . They are short on staff because it's not dinnertime yet. . . . She's not sure if they deliver to this location. . . . Other workers are too busy to help her. . . . The two new pizzas they had been advertising are no longer available. . . . We need to order something else instead. . . . Someone is helping her with the order. . . . She doesn't know how to take a credit card payment. . . . Can we pay with cash?"

More than eight minutes after dialing the restaurant, Randy reported the order was finally completed. An imperfect storm of operational problems had converted the seemingly simple task of ordering three pizzas into a painful adventure. Eight minutes . . . enough time to bake ten Totino's Pizza Rolls.[2] I suspect that the average customer on a typical pizza occasion would have given up long before.

After our orders were delivered, we experienced what pizza does best—bringing people together. In a multigenerational conversation, we mingled as we ate, sharing perspectives on the finer points of America's favorite food. I was pleased with how the multigenerational encounter had unfolded.

A half hour later, our young guests returned to their parents, and our president asked that we take a few minutes to debrief on our interaction with the teens. Generally positive comments were shared regarding the experience, but when it came time for our chief financial officer to speak, he looked at me and said, "Now I understand what you have been talking about, Larry. We need to do a better job with our telephone ordering process."

I was stunned. I recall thinking to myself, "Here is the most numbers-oriented person on the team . . . whom I have been showing hard data pointing to this issue for months . . . but he needed to see and experience the problem in order to believe it?"

Then it hit me—*that was the point!* Lifeless, abstract data had not persuaded him, but a real-life, albeit amplified, dramatization of what could go wrong with a pizza order had allowed him to persuade himself. I imagine that our CFO, a seasoned professional proud of our company, found it painful to be a spectator while a miserable customer experience unfolded before his eyes. But I suspect the experience added an emotional component to his understanding and compelled him, for perhaps the first time in his career, to see our business through the eyes of our customers rather than see our customers through the eyes of the business.

In the months ahead, the CFO became an advocate for initiatives to improve the customer experience in all aspects of our pizza-ordering process. His surprising change in position made me realize that representing the "voice of the customer" demanded more than PowerPoint presentations loaded with facts and data. I realized more persuasive insight could be generated by having our leaders spend time with our consumers than by showing them reams of quantitative data. I began to see my role as a consumer-insight professional to be less about attempting to sway management based on my interpretation of the data and more about facilitating experiences that took them out of their offices to engage with customers as they faced real-life challenges.

This *show instead of tell* principle applies far beyond the world of business or the craft of advertising. It is also pertinent to matters of everyday life, such as getting our children to brush their teeth or convincing family members to spend their vacation working on a service project. When we feel we are not being heard, it is easy to place the blame on others. However, the burden falls as much or more on the communicator to find ways to get others to persuade themselves.

---

[1] John Hughes' film credits include National Lampoon's *Vacation* (1983) and its sequels, National Lampoon's *European Vacation* (1985) and National Lampoon's *Christmas Vacation* (1989); *Mr. Mom* (1983); *Sixteen Candles* (1984); *Weird Science* (1985); *The Breakfast Club* (1985); *Ferris Bueller's Day Off* (1986); *Pretty in Pink* (1986); *Some Kind of Wonderful* (1987); *Planes, Trains and Automobiles* (1987); *She's Having a Baby* (1988); *Uncle Buck* (1989); *Dutch* (1991); *Dennis the Menace* (1993); *Baby's Day Out* (1994); and *Home Alone* (1990) and its sequels, *Home Alone 2: Lost in New York* (1992) and *Home Alone 3* (1997).

[2] Lisa Owens, "27 things you can do in 8 minutes and 46 seconds," *Beneath the Surface News* (blog), June 16, 2020, https://www.beneaththesurfacenews.com/post/27-things-you-can-do-in-8-minutes-and-46-seconds.

Chapter Twenty

Circle the Wagons

As fans funneled their way through the narrow stadium entrance, little did they know they were about to witness a game that is still talked about fifty years later. Capping off a weekend of reunions and parties, students and alumni were eager to grab the best bleacher seats they could find in anticipation of the big game. The Augustana Vikings had manhandled the Carroll Pioneers two months earlier by a whopping forty-five-point margin. Despite that lopsided defeat, fans there to celebrate Carroll's Alumni Night were wondering the same thing: Was there any possibility their home squad could pull off a major upset of a small college powerhouse from Illinois?

The Pioneers came close. The final tally was Augustana 12, Carroll 6, a score that looks like one from a football game where kickers from both teams either missed all their extra points or made a lot of field goals. But these conference foes played a different kind of game that night, one that both challenged my understanding of what *competition* looked like and offered a lesson about properly defining *success*.

I was one of the thousand or so packed inside Carroll's Van Male Field House on a Saturday evening in early February 1973, enjoying a front-row seat as color commentator for Augustana's college radio station, WVIK. A fraternity brother had handed off the nonpaying gig to me prior to the start of the season. I had played on Augie's freshman squad the year before, but chronic back problems had led to my decision to give up playing the sport I loved. Announcing varsity games provided a way to stay connected to basketball and enjoy a courtside view of a Viking team destined for greatness during the 1972–73 season.

I had no public speaking experience to prepare me for announcing a fast-action sporting event, so I was delighted when my predecessor shared this useful advice: "There will be times during a game when you might find it difficult to think of something to say," he said. "When that happens, just talk about *momentum*, how one team is gaining it or the other is losing it. Either way, it's always there. So, when in doubt, talk about *momentum*." This simple advice rescued me on numerous occasions.

I never had a chance to lean on this color commentator's best friend during this game of mismatched opponents. No one was surprised when the Vikings converted the opening tip-off of this rematch into a basket twenty seconds into the game. On Carroll's first offensive possession, their point guard stopped just past half court and stuffed the ball under his right armpit while three teammates weaved around a perimeter fifteen to twenty feet from the basket. I shared a glance with my play-by-play partner, Mike, who was looking for me to say something that would help our listening audience back on campus understand why we were failing to report any action. "They're just looking for open shots," I suggested.

Within seconds I realized my mistake. The Pioneers weren't looking for *any* shots. They were in a complete stall, a tactic possible before the forty-five-second shot clock was instituted in men's basketball before the 1985–86 season. Carroll teammates passed the ball back and forth with an occasional dribble or two thrown in for good measure. The referees, rendered purposeless by the lack of action, took on the role of spectators.

On the other end of the court, the Viking's fiery coach's face grew redder by the moment as the Carroll cagers showed no interest in scoring. Augustana's nationally ranked team, which had entered the weekend averaging an impressive eighty points per game, was being denied the opportunity to do what they did best—put up big numbers in an era when there was no shot clock or three-point field goal option.

The game dragged on like an uncomfortable blind date. Taking advantage of Pioneer turnovers, the Viking offense converted five of nine shot attempts, while Carroll made only one of three—a breakaway layup immediately following one Augustana basket. After the clock ticked down with few interruptions, the scoreboard read Augustana 10, Carroll 2 at halftime.

Augustana used their initial possession of the second half as a teachable moment for their opponent. The Viking point guard brought the ball past half court, stopped, and tucked it under his arm, mirroring Carroll's initial possession in the first half. The message from the Augustana bench was clear: *If you don't want to play this game, we don't need to play either. We're ahead by eight points. Should we just end this and go home early?* After pausing the action for precisely one minute, enough to make the point, the Vikings returned to running their motion offense designed around a continuous series of screens and cuts that, when executed with patience, routinely led to an open shot. With 18:45 remaining, Augustana scored to give the Vikings a 12-2 lead.

On their next possession, Carroll returned the game to the same deliberate pace, passing up shots even when invited to by a sagging Viking defense. Meanwhile, the hundred Augie supporters who had traveled to Wisconsin expressed their displeasure with vocal mockery of each meaningless move the Pioneers made. As their chants of "Bounce. Bounce. Pass. Bounce. Pass. Pass" echoed throughout the gym, home fans sat in stoic silence.

Throughout the second half, Augustana's coaches implemented a variety of defensive schemes, more likely intended to keep their players engaged than to stymie a Pioneer offense showing no interest in scoring. Then, to everyone's surprise, Carroll scored consecutive baskets within a three-minute span, narrowing the score to 12 to 6 with eleven minutes remaining in the game. With their team down by six points, Carroll fans anticipated a flurry of action calculated to achieve an upset of stunning proportions—quick shots on offense, a pressing defense trying for a steal, intentional fouls of frustrated Viking players who might miss crucial free throws, a full-out bid to win.

Nothing close to that happened in the final eight minutes. The Carroll squad attempted only two field goals and committed only two fouls, neither of which forced a Viking free throw. Their final shot with ninety seconds remaining was blocked by the Vikings' center, giving Augustana possession and allowing them to run out the clock. As time expired, the scoreboard read the same as it had with eleven minutes remaining: Augustana 12, Carroll 6 (a score so unusual one Chicago newspaper added a parenthetical comment "correct score" in their publication the next day).

As time expired, any hopeful energy that had filled Van Male Field House before tip-off escaped from the space like the last gasp of air from a balloon collapsing in on itself. Augustana's coach approached Carroll's coach and said, "You didn't try to win!"

"We held you to only twelve points" was his response. Perhaps that was the goal from the onset—to achieve historic lows.[1] If that was the case, Carroll's strategy was a "success." Six points scored by one team, and the eighteen-point combined total, are both record lows in the modern history of college basketball.[2] No substitutes played, and only two players from each team scored. No free throws were attempted during the entire game.

Those are the facts. But a nagging feeling of being robbed of something undefined that night remained with me until I happened upon a book investigating the impact of mindset on athletic performance. In *Top Dog: The Science of Winning and Losing*, sports psychologists Po

Bronson and Ashley Merryman examined the fifth (and final) shootout kicks used to determine the winner of a soccer game ending in a tie. When a missed kick would result in a *loss*, professional players converted 62 percent of their shots. But when a successful kick would result in a *win*, players scored 92 percent of the time. Since all the shots were identical in terms of target and distance, the 30 percent point difference demonstrates how the odds of success improve dramatically when the competition is framed as the potential to *win* versus the possibility to *lose*.[3]

The Carroll coaching staff did not have the benefit of that 2008 research, but they must have understood that lacking the motivation to win, their players would accept failure as a satisfactory outcome. While we can never know what might have happened if Carroll coaches had not chosen to "circle the wagons" and define *success* as a respectable loss in front of alumni, we can be certain that framing those final minutes as an opportunity to win would have improved their chances.

There is a danger lurking behind diminished expectations that extends beyond the arena of competitive sports. It applies to our everyday interactions with family, friends, and colleagues as well. The lesson here is this: Regardless of your role, defining what *success* looks like is a critical leadership responsibility because the result you demand is the result you are likely to get.

---

[1] In the interest of fairness and accuracy, with the help of the Carroll College Sports Information Department, I was able to interview one player from the Carroll team. He confirmed stalling was the planned strategy but claimed "no recollection of throwing in the towel" at the end of the game. While I respect his version of events, archival information, multiple newspaper articles, and statements from many attending the game supported my recollection that Carroll made no viable attempt to win the game.

[2] According to www.reference.com, the lowest final score for a college basketball game was 12 to 10 in a game between Duke and North Carolina State in 1968. Perhaps they fail to include small college contests in their record-keeping. The February 1973 Augustana-Carroll game does remain the record for the College Conference of Illinois and Wisconsin (CCIW). Acknowledgement: My deepest appreciation goes to the Sports Information Department at Augustana College, for providing me with archival information and newspaper articles regarding this game. These documents supported my recollection that Carroll did not attempt to win the game, while adding and correcting some details of the contest I had either forgotten or misremembered.

[3] Po Bronson and Ashley Merryman, *Top Dog: The Science of Winning and Losing* (New York City: Twelve, 2014).

Chapter Twenty-One

A Critical Distinction

I had never been as prepared for a meeting in my career, or so I thought. My assignment was to lead the discussion that day, but any illusion I held about being in control of the conversation vanished within the first five minutes. Fortunately, a man of wisdom was there, ready to rescue me.

It was my seventh year working with the Gatorade team as director of marketing information, and I had recently been assigned a role I'd designed for myself. I wouldn't call it a *dream job*, but it represented a personal development opportunity and reflected what I thought was right for our business. The idea was to migrate strategic planning from a financial exercise to one driven by our agreed-upon assumptions regarding the marketplace challenges that would define our brand's future. This would be accomplished through ongoing discussions intended to align our senior team on questions that could fundamentally impact the way we did business in the years ahead: When should we take price increases? How would we protect our brand in the face of emerging competition? Should we expand our product into new channels of distribution? Under this approach, strategy development would be an issue-driven year-round activity with one leadership team meeting each month devoted to a crucial topic. My role would be to present information to frame and inform these discussions.

Coming into the initial meeting, I knew the stakes were high. Some members of the leadership team had expressed skepticism regarding the approach. They believed these discussions would distract from more immediate business concerns. It would be more efficient, they argued, to handle strategic planning as a point-in-time exercise fit into the annual corporate timeline.

While my background in research and analysis made me a good fit for information-gathering aspects of the role, I had reservations about whether I was seasoned enough to lead a meeting with eight senior members of the management team. Peggy, my boss at the time, suggested we engage a veteran marketing consultant who was familiar with the business to help facilitate the discussion. Dave was highly respected by the senior team, including our newly appointed division president.

The plan going into the meeting would be for me to provide the substance while Dave would jump in to lead as needed. The session got off to a solid start when the president kicked things off with supportive comments regarding this initial foray into the new process. But then, seemingly out of nowhere, an organizational "gunfight" erupted, with verbal shots being fired from all angles inside the conference room. Despite the passage of time and the limitations of memory, I recall a heated exchange that went something like this:

President: "Before we get started with our new strategy process, are there any pressing issues we need to discuss?"

Functional Leader #1: "I have concerns about our plans to introduce the new product next quarter. I don't think it's ready for market."

Functional Leader #2: "We debated that at our last staff meeting, and it seemed everyone was on board with the decision to go ahead with the launch."

Functional Leader #1: "Well, I went back to my team, and they told me they don't support this because of supply chain issues. So neither do I."

Functional Leader #2: "Which is it? That the product isn't ready or because of the supply chain?"

Functional Leader #3: "What difference does it make? My team isn't aligned with us launching the product either."

Functional Leader #4: "I recall that we all agreed at the last meeting. Why didn't either of you raise your concerns then?"

Functional Leader #1: "I don't remember agreeing."

Functional Leader #2: "Yes, you did. We went through the test market results, which demonstrate this new product has the sales potential to help us achieve our profit plan for the year. You told us that your team could address the supply chain issues through focused attention on it."

Functional Leader #1: "My team just doesn't have the resources to handle it now."

I had no idea what I might say in this tense moment. I sat in stunned silence. I wanted to duck for cover and avoid getting caught in the verbal cross fire, but there was no place to hide. I had never witnessed well-respected leaders express discord in this manner. Something was operating beneath the surface that had moved these colleagues from discussion to argument. My hope for a successful initial strategic planning meeting was slipping away, being replaced by heated debate that continued:

President: "Well, I should tell you all that [Functional Leader #1] came to my office after our last meeting and shared his concerns with me in private. He made some valid points. So as president, I wanted to open this meeting by giving him an opportunity to revisit our decision."

Functional Leader #5: "That's not right! We already had this discussion!"

Functional Leader #6: "Yes. What's the deal? Everyone agreed!"

Functional Leader #1: "Not all of us!"

Functional Leader #4: "This happens all of the time. We have discussions and seem to reach a consensus, but then, after the meeting, someone goes to [President] and gets him to change his mind. It's frustrating because not only do we waste time, but I am never sure we are all pulling in the same direction."

Functional Leader #5: "Yes. That's our organizational oxymoron. There is no such thing as a 'final decision' here!"

At this point Dave, who had been seated in the corner a few feet away from the table, stood and cleared his throat. Having the attention of the team, he proceeded to share what I believe was the most cogent commentary I heard in my entire corporate career.

Dave: "I know each of you possesses great passion for this business. That is a wonderful gift, which I hope you never lose. But it strikes me that, at times like this one, you may be allowing your personal opinions to get in the way of the greater good. The discussion that took place over the past few minutes is an example. I think this team is confusing two concepts: 'Agreement' versus 'support.'"

President: "What do you mean by that?"

Dave: "In business, there is a time to examine the data, discuss what it means, debate alternative courses of action, and reach a decision. Not everyone will *agree* with every decision, but those disagreements need to stay in this room once that decision has been made. The entire team must place the good of the group over their individual opinions and commit to *support* the decision. That's what great teams do! And it is the president's responsibility to hold everyone on his team to that standard.

"I challenge you, individually and as a team, to learn how to *support* a decision whether you *agree* with it or not, because if you don't, you are likely to get bogged down in debates that will paralyze the business and undermine your trust in each other."

Dave had saved the day. Not only had he defused the tension in the room, but he had offered a decision-making principle I could take with me for the rest of my life. He sensitized me to a distinction I had never considered before: the difference between *agreement* and *support*.

* * *

I discovered that supporting actions with which I don't agree is easier in principle than in practice. Nearly thirty years later, I was confronted with a situation that required a great deal of reflection to work through this support-without-agreement quandary. The details are not important here, but it involved a major initiative being considered by the church I had attended for the past twenty-plus years—to add a new worship service.

While I backed the notion that new expression of worship was the right thing for our church at this critical phase in its history, I did not agree with the way an outside consultant was using survey and focus group research (tools I had used my entire career to gain insight and understanding) to "help the congregation see" this was a good idea. My thoughts on how to reorient our research efforts toward learning instead of persuasion were met with resistance. When I sensed my suggestions were hurting more than helping our working group move forward, I resigned from the team.

But I still faced a personal dilemma: how to reconcile my disagreement with the approach with support for the direction. To get there, I worked through a series of questions that moved me to a position of unequivocal support for the idea.

Q. Did I have an opportunity to share my point of view with our team?

A. Yes. Since I had my chance to influence the outcome, it became easier for me to accept the team's decision.

Q. Do I understand the rationale that was used to arrive at the decision?

A. Yes. I see significant benefits associated with the direction we will be taking. I took issue with the process used, not the outcome.

Q. Is it clear how this decision can lead to something positive once it has been executed?

A. Yes. Something good may lie ahead for our church at the end of the journey. It is more important that the organization succeeds by pursuing this initiative than it is for me to win an argument during a committee meeting.

Q. Do I have any legal or moral or ethical concerns regarding the direction that is being set?

A. No, but if I did, that would be a red flag, and I would need to consider whether I wanted to remain a part of this organization.

Q. Can I trust my leaders to do what they believe is the right thing for the organization?

A. Yes. That is why they were selected to be in this leadership position.

Q. Will I commit to doing everything in my power to make this a success?

A. Yes. In fact, I will have to work even harder to make it happen so that I leave no doubt that I am supportive. The worst thing that could happen would be for me to be viewed as trying to undermine its success.

***

There will always be differences of opinion, which is a good thing. A well-known saying (incorrectly attributed to Winston Churchill) says it well: "If two people agree on everything, one of them is unnecessary."

Agreement and *support* are not the same thing. Once the debating is over and the decision has been made, everyone must find a way to get behind it. Working through a series of questions like the ones shared here may offer a viable path to get there.

Learning to distinguish between the two requires a mental muscle that takes time and effort to build. But doing so is critical to maintaining valued bonds with teammates, family members, or friends. It becomes easier to do so when we recognize that there is almost always something more important at stake than the decision at hand, like your commitment to a cause, an enterprise, or relationships you value.

Chapter Twenty-Two

Bend but Don't Break

Her slumped shoulders, her downward gaze, her sullen face—images that told the story of a battle waged but lost.

I was standing in the Emergency Department hallway of a large children's hospital when the nurse made her exit from critical care unit 2. I could only imagine the scene on the other side of the door as she, along with a team of doctors and other nurses, worked in the middle of the night to save the life of a three-month-old child injured in an automobile accident. Despite their heroic efforts, they did not succeed.

As the nurse exited, she glanced my way and said, "You have the toughest job in the hospital." In my gut I knew this was far from the truth. I could never handle what she and her colleagues did every day, bringing the best medical knowledge and treatments to life-and-death emergencies.

"We all have tough jobs here," I replied in a feeble attempt to acknowledge the challenging nature of her work. She nodded slightly and walked away, leaving me to face the sobering assignment that lay ahead: guiding a family through the initial stages of their grieving process in the aftermath of an infant's death.

There had been countless moments over the prior four months when I'd puzzled over how I had arrived here as a chaplain only years after my corporate career ending. The history was straightforward enough: I had been bringing my guitar and my voice here for three years as a therapeutic musician. It had become easier to enter the room of a severely ill child, read the situation, and select an appropriate song. The sight of the sickest of children bothered me less with time, but the sense of fulfillment I felt while serving others through my music had begun to wane. I began to feel these children needed more than a single song and that maybe I did too. In the fall of 2012, I started my eight-month commitment in the Pastoral Care Department at a large metropolitan area children's hospital. It was an assignment I expected would be a natural extension of what I was already doing through my music. I was wrong.

On the first day of my chaplaincy, I entered a world unrecognizable to me. I may have walked into the same building via the pedestrian skybridge I had become familiar with through the years, but that was where the similarities ended. I was surprised when my photo ID badge read *chaplain*, with *intern* conspicuously absent. When a fellow CPE colleague and I protested because we had neither the experience nor training to justify that title, our supervisor explained that we would not have been trusted in the role if we couldn't do the job. He likened our concern about a lack of know-how to the Cowardly Lion character in *The Wizard of Oz*. "His search was to find the lion already inside of him," our supervisor said. "Each of you is on a journey to find the chaplain already within you based on your life experiences." Neither of us bought into the metaphor at the time.

A few weeks into the assignment, I began to feel more comfortable in the role. I learned how to abide the emotional pain felt by others and listen to questions that had no answers. I prayed out loud more than I had in any period in my life. I learned to recognize when the situation outran my competency and, more importantly, where to find the resources that were needed in the moment. And on that painful night when the nurse acknowledged the challenge that I would face, I rose to the task, held myself together through the darkest of nights, and offered a grieving mother the comfort and support she needed until well after the sun rose the next morning.

I came to realize I would not be applying for permanent citizenship in this world where suffering and existential doubt abided. During our final session together, one of my peers said something that caught my attention: "This is not a job. It is more of a calling. If one has no passion or calling for this role, then one will not be effective, nor will they last." He was not talking about me per se, but his comment spoke to my self-assessment at the end of my eight-month commitment to the role: I was not built to last as a chaplain.

I also knew deep inside that my eight-month passage through the world of pastoral care had been worth it. My unit of CPE training provided some of the most enriching experiences of my life. I had been invited into situations I could never have imagined and met wonderful people on what might have been the worst day of their lives. I felt a deeper connection to humankind than ever before. I saw more, felt more, and learned more about life and death and pain and the needs of others than I had during any experience in my previous sixty years on this earth. I learned to listen for what was being communicated behind the spoken words. I became aware of my biases and beliefs, the "personal potholes" I needed to navigate around to be fully present for others. I discovered I could be a calm presence for families in difficult moments. I stood by, walked with, and sat in the presence of others in their times of great pain. I managed to hold together through it all. I grasped that one can only "pastor" out of who they genuinely are, and I believe I did this. The stress I experienced in this new world changed me for the better by providing me with the resilience I might need to endure future hardships.

My personal learning about gaining strength through stress is like what scientists discovered about trees planted in Biosphere 2, a miniature domed model of our planet built in Southern Arizona beginning in 1987. The goal for Biosphere 2 was to investigate whether a closed ecosystem could support and maintain life in outer space. The trees planted inside the dome grew quickly at first but collapsed under their own weight before reaching maturity. The problem: there was no wind inside the dome. The stress that wind places on trees in nature is critical to their survival. Wind strengthens cellular structure, enabling the tree to handle more challenging forces it will face in the future.

The same concept applies to our everyday lives. We get accustomed to, maybe complacent in, the world around us. When we enter a new one, however, assumptions get thrown up for grabs. We become challenged by a new set of norms, different rules of behavior, a unique spoken language, new principles governing success. We learn to flex new emotional muscles that give us the strength we need to grow. I can see now that **my passage through the world of pastoral care produced emotional headwinds that bent and shaped me. I didn't break under the raw humanity I witnessed there, and I emerged stronger on the other end.**

My challenge to you is to *explore new worlds* and situations that will test your limits and awaken your spirit. I have more in mind here than a two-week vacation in Paris or a trip to Machu Picchu. Maybe it's taking on a new responsibility at work, volunteering for a cause you know little about, taking a Zumba class, pursuing a new career, or climbing a tree. You be the judge. Based on my experience, I suspect that **by pushing yourself beyond your comfort zone, you will discover you are capable of more than you ever imagined and become a better version of yourself as a result.**

Chapter Twenty-Three

The Move You Don't Make

I sensed something was troubling Michael by the way he hovered at my office doorway. He didn't knock, nor did he enter. He just stood there in limbo. I invited him in to take a seat.

Across the table from me, Michael's furrowed brow signaled a more serious discussion ahead than I usually enjoyed with my affable colleague. We made small talk for a minute or so before he moved to the real reason for his visit. "I don't know what my future is here." I nodded my understanding.

With that single comment, Michael had gifted me with a coachable moment, a chance to share from my own experience with career path doubt. I thought back to ten or so years earlier, when I had been discouraged over the trajectory of my career. "Let me tell you about the time I had a similar feeling and what I learned in the process," I said. "I held a position leading marketing insights and strategy at Gatorade, which was experiencing tremendous sales growth. The brand was the crown jewel in the Quaker Oats portfolio and poised to expand around the globe. After working on it for nine years, I knew the business and the senior executives who ran it very well. From any objective perspective, I should have been content, even delighted, with my situation.

"I wasn't certain exactly what was stirring inside, but I had contracted an itch no salve could relieve. Maybe it was a title I sought, acknowledgment of past contributions, or recognition of future potential. With a global expansion on the horizon, I envisioned an assignment that would make me a vital part of a worldwide brand team. I shared that idea with my supportive supervisor, who in turn raised it with the division president. 'That is not something in our plans,' he said, shutting down that discussion and my career dreaming.

"Over the next few months, I slipped into an increasingly pessimistic approach to the difficult task of career management. I stewed over something that was never promised to me. Self-perceived slights began to pile up into a mountain of discontent, which became increasingly difficult to climb over. I became impatient. I began to feel trapped in the same discussions I'd had years earlier with a different set of colleagues. What I should have embraced as an opportunity to share my knowledge with new teammates devolved into a 'been here, done this' attitude. Instead of moving forward, I stalled."

"So, what happened?" asked Michael. "Obviously, you didn't stay, because you've been here at Pizza Hut a few years."

"That's true, but I took a job at another company before I came here. It was a lateral move in terms of title but represented a sizable increase in both annual budget and the staff. They wanted me, which fed my ego. The job was in the same city, so there was no need to disrupt my family with a move. But the icing on the cake was that the role reflected a new functional mission espoused by the hiring manager: to elevate the role and impact of marketing information in decision-making. I saw this as an opportunity to have an impact by applying what I had learned during my prior ten years in a new and exciting context.

"It took me less than a month to realize I had made a terrible mistake. I discovered that my expanded responsibilities distanced me from the day-to-day business decisions of the five brand groups my team supported. In this highly matrixed organizational structure, I sat perched in the crosshairs of a longstanding battle between my solid-line and dotted-line bosses. I spent my days feeling isolated in bureaucratic purgatory, where I either represented the division's interests in functional meetings or the marketing information function's perspective in division meetings. The role left little leeway to make unique contributions.

"I observed a great deal of organizational politics in that year and discovered I despised it. I longed to be back at my old job. But I also realized it was impossible to go back, because that meant denying my reasons for leaving in the first place. More on point, I understood that companies are adept at moving on, and I was now just part of their history. I was realizing the veracity of hypothetical discussions with one former colleague where we contrasted how important we felt we were to the organization with the realization that the company would find it easy to replace us. 'We're fungible,' Jackie would say. 'Like any other resource that can be bought or sold, we are easily replaced.'

"It was during that difficult year that I was able to gain clarity on the essential mistake I had made in leaving Gatorade: when considering a job change, make sure you have a compelling reason pulling you to a new position and not just a lot of little things pushing you away from the current one.

"Michael, I know things aren't perfect here, but the grass is not always greener somewhere else. You are highly thought of and someone who is considered to have great long-term potential in this company. Let's work together to identify some options. Ultimately, only you can determine what is best for you. But I want you to apply what I learned as you make your decision."

A couple of months after our talk, Michael took a job at another company, which did not work out for him. He eventually found a work situation where he has been extremely successful, for which I am thankful.

I wonder now if I provided Michael with the advice he needed that day. I painted an accurate picture of why a previous job change had not been a good choice for me. But I spent so much time telling my story that I left little time for Michael to share his. I used a worn-out cliché that made my story narrative like recycled junk. If I had the chance for a do-over, I would frame up the need for Michael to "run toward" something and then spend our time together exploring what the right destination looked like for him.

***

When you feel like you are stuck in a situation, you see no clear path going forward, and problems keep piling up, it is natural to focus on the negatives and look for an escape route. The danger here is pursuing change for change's sake may simply place you in a different situation where you are likely to encounter the same problems that plagued you in the past. Avoid running away, because it is a backward-looking approach that seldom works.

"Running toward" begins with a clear understanding of where you are today and where you hope to be tomorrow. It is a forward-looking approach that requires developing a vision of your future that can provide guidance as you navigate your way forward. The challenge here, however, is that this demands a great deal of work up front to align what you want out of your life and career with the myriad of possibilities this world has to offer. "Running toward" is much harder than "running away," which is why it is usually the path less taken.

We all have many different relationships—as an employee, a member of an organization, a partner in a marriage—but I think the same cautionary principle applies. When a lot of small issues are leading you toward making a significant change to a relationship, stop and consider whether you are in fact "running toward" something that will make things better off in the long run. Weigh your options carefully because sometimes the best move is the one you don't make.

Chapter Twenty-Four

It's a Derba

The morning drizzle would not discourage our plan on the final weekend of our three-week

vacation in the Netherlands. Sandy and I both felt a void. It was time to go to church.

Worshipping each Sunday morning had become woven into the moral fabric of our thirty-

year marriage, and the church spire on the other side of the Oudegracht ("old canal") from our

Airbnb was inviting us to check it out. We hoped for a worship experience here might tie us back

to the Dutch Reformed Church tradition in which we had both been raised.

Utrecht was a good place to seek out this connection since the city has been the religious

center of the Netherlands since the Middle Ages. This position of importance was apparent as we

stood outside Jacobikerk, an imposing brown-brick gothic structure erected by Catholics near the

close of the thirteenth century. Inside, we encountered a cavernous sanctuary characteristic of

hall church design, where the side aisles are about the same height as the central nave. The walls

were devoid of primary colors. (I learned later that after Jacobikerk was handed over to the

Protestants following the Reformation in the late 1500s, they removed religious icons from the

altar and whitewashed the walls.) I could imagine how radiant this space might feel on mornings

when sunlight bathed the entire sanctuary. But not on this Sunday, as the clear leaded windows

freed the outdoor gloom to permeate this vast space.

The locals gave us a cordial welcome in English and handed us each a copy of the worship

bulletin printed in Dutch. Within minutes the service began, following the familiar formalities of

Christian worship, albeit in a foreign language. We participated as best we could, reminded of

our communication barrier at every step on the liturgy—prayers, congregational singing, scripture readings. When the pastor made announcements, the congregation sat in stoic silence. I was not looking forward to the next item in the order of worship—the sermon offered in a language that I would not understand. I settled in, anticipating the half hour of daydreaming ahead, hoping some spiritual presence would drift into my unengaged being.

In an instant, everything changed. During the brief pause between the pastor's announcements and the sermon, a dozen or so children ages five to eight popped up from locations scattered throughout the sanctuary. They skipped and jumped, giggled and laughed their way along the wide aisle to our left. Sounds of glee echoed throughout the sanctuary as they burst toward an exit in the back. It was like a joyous jailbreak, no doubt fueled by their delight in being pardoned from the boredom their parents had, through years of practice, come to passively accept as worship.

A moment later, they were gone, returning the space to silence and leaving me wondering: Where does that natural sense of delight children express come from? Why do we lose it as we age? What can I, as an adult, do to regain that childlike exuberance?

Looking for answers, I decided to follow the advice I had given to former colleagues in my presentation on "25 Things I Learned in 25 Years in Business": Hang out with Kids.[1] I had been helping lead Sunday school music with the children at my church for ten years, but I made a commitment to do more. I volunteered to teach ukulele at the annual arts and music summer day camp. I agreed to monitor recreation time during Vacation Bible School, where I let them take the lead (except for setting boundaries to protect their safety) and just stayed out of the way. I allowed them to do what children do best—play. I observed as they created imaginary worlds with familiar objects. They invited me to participate, to literally get down on the floor with them, which I did.

At a family breakfast to kick off the new Sunday school year, I sat with three six-year-olds as they answered get-to-know-each-other questions like the name of their pet or their favorite activity. As they worked on an assignment to draw an image from nature, I watched them build on each other's ideas without judgment. Each offered suggestions for new details of the creature they were imagining together. When it was finished, I was curious about the long-eared, pink-and-blue-striped animal with four thick legs that appeared to have small balls on the bottom of each foot.

"What is that?" I asked.

"It's a derba," answered Emma with impressive confidence.

"What's a derba?" I asked.

"It's like a zebra, except it has wheels on its legs so it can go really fast and win the derby," explained James without hesitating.

"Well, of course," I replied. "That makes perfect sense."

Sensing their answers satisfied my adult curiosity, they moved on to the next activity, leaving me to study their original work of art capturing this new animal species.

What I saw in that fleeting moment of imagination was the creative expression that flows naturally in children, called by some a *beginner's mind*. In Zen Buddhism, this concept is known as *shoshin* and refers to approaching a subject, even one familiar to you, with an attitude of openness. When you are a beginner at something, which happens to children much of the time, you are more open to new information and possibilities. As a result, children tend to be more sensitive and connected to their environment than adults.

Scientific research confirms that children (four-to-five-year-olds) are adept at noticing things adults may miss.[2] Because of their natural curiosity, children pay greater attention to all the information presented to them. They may not be as good at focusing as adults, but kids excel at learning in unfamiliar settings because they take in more information. Adults exhibit selective attention, making them superior at capturing information they are expected to remember while ignoring the rest. Children tend to see it all.

We don't need a scientific journal article to validate what can be observed in public shopping malls or parks. The next time you find yourself in one of these places, pay attention to how young children navigate the space compared to their parents. Chances are you will see them stopping often to look up, down, all around while the adults remain focused straight ahead. Children are innately more curious about the world that surrounds them and, as a result, find it easier to delight in God's creation.

Can that sense of wonder, the beginner's mind, be completely recaptured? I doubt it. It doesn't look like anyone is going to discover a mythical spring able to restore youth to anyone who drinks from it anytime soon. But growing up doesn't have to mean slipping into fascination fatigue. Hanging out with kids and making play a deliberate activity can help adults *rediscover the powerful sense of wonder* that comes so naturally to children. All we have to do is trust them, let them lead the exploration, reserve our judgment, and throw ourselves into whatever imaginary world they invite us into. Letting our children be our teachers allows us to experience again what it is like to have that beginner's mind, open to new possibilities. Spending time with children allows you to get in touch with your inner child . . . that carefree version you wish you could be today.

***

As we rose to sing the final hymn that Sunday morning at Jacobikerk, I caught the children out of the corner of my eye making their joyous return. The scene brightened as they skipped and jumped, giggled and laughed, making their way along the wide aisle on our left. Echoes of joy returned to the vast sanctuary as they returned to their parents. I noticed each was holding papers in their hand, most likely a craft designed to help them understand the Sunday school lesson of the day. Or perhaps it was the product of their God-given creative spirit, something extraordinary and new like a derba. I hope so.

---

[1] See the full list of "25 Things" in the appendix.
[2] Vladimir Sloutsky and Daniel Plebanek, "Costs of Selective Attention: When Children Notice What Adults Miss," *Psychological Science* 28, no. 6 (April 2017): 723–732, https://doi.org/10.1177/0956797617693005.

Summary of Part III

Lessons I Have Learned from my Relationship with the World Around Me

- ➢ Take initiative. If something is not working, stop complaining, and work toward fixing it.

- ➢ Slow down. Since a lifetime consists of a series of brief moments, making each one matter will make our lives matter more as a result.

- ➢ Show instead of tell. Look for ways to help others persuade themselves.

- ➢ Define success. This leadership responsibility is critical because the result you demand is the result you are likely to get.

- ➢ Find a way to support. Even if you don't agree, once the debating is over and the decision has been made, commit to supporting it.

- ➢ Explore new worlds. Entering unfamiliar places and situations can test your limits, awaken your spirit, and reveal that you are capable of more than you imagined.

- ➢ Run toward. When considering a major change, be sure you have a compelling reason to make that move. Avoid letting little things that bother you push you away from the current situation.

- ➢ Rediscover wonder. Spend time with children because it allows you to recapture the mind of a beginner, open to new possibilities.

Part IV: Transcendent Power

I believe in God. I always have. This foundational religious tenet was impressed upon me by my parents and the Protestant Dutch community where I was raised. His or her existence was consistently affirmed as an abiding truth throughout my youth.

While most Americans share my view on this matter, belief in God is about as trendy as having a telephone landline. A recent Gallup poll found 81 percent responded *yes* to the simple question "Do you believe in God?"—a record low compared to the 96 percent who agreed in 1944, the first year the question was asked in their survey.[1]

I suspect this finding troubles our Lord, providing another data point contributing to what must be an all-time-low holy approval rating for humankind. The collective damage we continue to levy on God's creation makes Adam and Eve's failure to abide by a couple of simple rules of paradise (and their subsequent "cover-up" involving fig leaves and lies) look like a minor transgression. What will it take for God to banish us from our earthly Eden? I wonder.

I digress. The stories in this section are not intended to sway anyone's view on the question of God's existence. Evangelism does not fit my nature and has always impressed me as a bit heavy-handed. The seeds of that view may have been planted when I attended a Billy Graham Crusade at the tender age of nine. Members of our tiny church community loaded into a yellow school bus for the one-hour trip north to the big city of Chicago. I was awestruck by the vast multitude (five thousand people) assembled inside the great hall of McCormick Place that night. While I do not recollect a word the great pastor (who earned the nickname "God's Machine Gun" because of his fast and thunderous speaking style) preached that evening, I recall being concerned someone from our group might answer the altar call and delay our return trip. It seems I was more worried about everyone getting home than anyone being saved that night. My practical concern turned out to be unwarranted. Everyone in our church group made it back to the bus on time.[2]

The stories in this section do not attempt to prove the existence of God, Yahweh, Allah, Supreme Being, Divine Presence, or whatever word you choose to name it. I accept this as a matter of personal choice. Rather, my goal is to share personal experiences that were initiated outside of me and where I sensed the presence of "something bigger" breaking through the mundane, grabbing my attention, and deepening my connection to the Transcendent Power. Together, they moved my understanding of God from the remote and judging being I was taught about as a child to an immediate living presence in my life today.

---

[1] Jeffrey M. Jones, "Belief in God in U.S. Dips to 81%, a New Low," Gallup News, June 17, 2022, Politics, https://news.gallup.com/poll/393737/belief-god-dips-new-low.aspx.

[2] When I shared this memory with my wife, who was also there that night, Sandy told me her mother's warning to avoid getting into the spirit of things and to head directly to the bus, not the altar, during the closing hymn.

Chapter Twenty-Five

The Tale of the Lost Trinket

Farming is, at its core, an exercise in controlling nature to reap a profit. No crop demanded more effort from its growers than the gladiolus, a flower raised by nearly every farmer in the rural community where I grew up seventy miles south of Chicago. Settled by Dutch immigrants in the late nineteenth century, unincorporated Wichert became a Midwest "glad" capital of sorts. Local farmers initially scratched out a living raising gladiolus bulbs but, in time, transitioned to the more profitable sale of the flowers they produced.

Unlike field corn and soybeans grown in the region, raising glads required year-round diligence. As the Midwestern winter gloom gave way to sunny days and the danger of frost passed, the rich soil warmed enough by May for planting thousands of these spherical bulbs (technically corms). Each was positioned upright by hand in a four-inch-deep trench and then buried under the earth. Within a few weeks, aided by irrigation and removal of invasive weeds such as crabgrass, green sword-shaped spikes would rise like soldiers standing at attention. Each one would be cut (by hand), then sorted and tied (by hand) into bundles of a dozen stems ready for sale. In the fall, the bulbs were removed from the ground (by hand) and placed in flat wooden crates to be stacked and stored in warehouses for drying. Midwinter, bulbs and the bulblets they produced were cleaned and sorted according to size (again by hand) and treated with fungicide in time for planting the next spring.

Wichert was a place where the proverb "You reap what you sow" was accepted as gospel truth. Buttressed by a Protestant ethic that viewed hard work as beneficial to both individuals and society, waking hours were directed toward productive goals. Sound farming practice centered around a horticultural principle that I accepted as absolute truth: every planted seed was expected to produce something of value.

***

Decades later and thousands of miles away from the Central Illinois plains, I encountered a cultivation approach that differs from the gladiolus paradigm in almost every way imaginable. On our sixth day walking the Camino de Santiago in Spain, Sandy and I had covered thirty kilometers by the time we reached a hostel run by Cistercian nuns in the small village of Santo Domingo de la Calzada. But instead of the calm air of hospitality that typically awaits pilgrims after a long day of walking, tension greeted us. Eva, a pilgrim from Canada we had met the day before, was pleading with two nuns standing in the tight passage that led past the front desk to the sleeping rooms. We learned that she had been assigned to quarters with a fireman and his wife from California. When he began snoring during his afternoon nap, Eva complained. The sisters asked them to move to a different room, a request that the couple mistook as a demand to find housing elsewhere.

As Sandy stepped in to translate the discussion between Eva and the nuns, the Californians arrived from inside carrying their backpacks. They stormed through the gauntlet to exit out the front door, and the man made a remark in his rudimentary Spanish to the nuns.

"That wasn't very nice," whispered Sandy to me. The faces of both nuns drooped. Their attempts to solve a problem had descended into conflict when their room-reassignment request was interpreted as an eviction notice.

The Camino offers many lessons, one of the most significant being tolerance for others. Sleeping in rooms with snoring strangers is part of the experience and one of the two greatest challenges one encounters when walking the Camino. (The other is foot-blister prevention and management.) Eva realized this fact and expressed regret to the sisters over her initial complaint. But it arrived too late, and her temporary roommates departed in a huff.

About a half hour later, after Sandy and I had showered and settled into our bunks to rest before dinner, the Mother Superior arrived in our room and began to speak to Sandy in Spanish. After thanking Sandy for her attempt to bridge the language gap and resolve the conflict, the nun reached into the pocket of her habit and pulled out four silver trinkets about the size of a nickel with the image of Jesus embossed on one side. "If you see the man again," she said, "give him one of these and tell him it is meant to invoke the love of Jesus."

When Sandy translated her assignment to me, I said, "Good luck with that. He was quite pissed!"

"Maybe we won't see him," Sandy replied.

An hour later, we were seated in a small café bar enjoying glasses of rioja wine and tapas when I noticed the couple pause near the entrance to study the menu posted outside.

"Hey, check it out," I said to Sandy. "They're here."

"Maybe they won't come in," she replied.

"What if they do? Will you give him the trinket?"

I didn't have to wait long for the answer as they entered and took a position at the bar next to us. As they studied their adult-beverage options, Sandy sprang into action. Honoring her assignment, she handed the trinket to the man and said, "I was asked by the nuns at the hostel to give this to you. They said this is meant to invoke the love of Jesus."

The man stared at the trinket resting in the palm of his large hand, contemplating its shape and the message delivered with it. After he'd paused a few seconds, his face reddened. He raised his arm high in the air, turned his hand downward, and slammed the trinket on the bar surface with a force that made the whole café shake. "They're the ones who need the spirit of Jesus, not me!" he exclaimed. He turned to his wife and said, "Let's go." They walked out the door, leaving the trinket and its stunned messenger behind.

Over the next few days, I lost track of the trinkets except for the one I had stashed away to give to Sandy later as a necklace. When we arrived in Santiago a couple of weeks later, Sandy and I ran into Eva again. As we chatted, Eva revealed that she had encountered the California couple a few days after the incident in a different town. She told us of her apology to the man for her intolerance for his snoring and the mix-up regarding the room assignments. Meanwhile, the man had shared that his career as a fireman contributed to upper respiratory issues that led to his snoring, a problem he was working to get under control.

As Eva shared this story, I noticed she had one of the silver trinkets around her wrist, held there by three or four loops of twine. Without my knowledge, Sandy had given it to Eva after the fireman had rejected it. The trinket had changed hands many times during its journey launched by the head nun, but having it end up on Eva's arm had not been part of the nun's plan, making Eva's possession of it both a mystery and miracle to me.

***

I suspect the Mother Superior had faith that the small token of peace she had placed in Sandy's hands would find its rightful place. I imagine the nun had given away hundreds of these small trinkets, never knowing for certain how or where her seeds of reconciliation might find fertile ground and grow into something positive. I am confident she held an unwavering belief that a force greater than her would be unleashed through its giving.

The faith of a Cistercian nun showed how some blessings in life can germinate and grow in ways beyond our imagination and control. Through her actions, she offered me a powerful alternative to the "planting" paradigm ingrained in me during my youth. Although it may not have represented practical farming practices, the way she "scattered" seeds of hope revealed an impressive spiritual one. In contrast to a planted bulb, a scattered seed follows its own trajectory and schedule, requires us to practice patience, forces us to abandon our facade of control, and demands a faith that somehow something good will result. "Scattering" is a superior service model because it values the seeds we sow over the harvest we reap.

In a world where measurable results define impact, it may be difficult to accept that some of our most important achievements in life may never be known to us. Job candidates don't include "I gave out a lot of trinkets to strangers this past year, but I don't know what happened to any of them" as a major accomplishment on their résumés. But that was how the Cistercian nun defined success. She scattered a seed and sent it on a mission unknown to her. She had faith that it would do its work once it left her hand. And it did.

While I haven't abandoned the planful principle of "planting," I have made it a priority to go out and *scatter seeds through good deeds*. That may take the form of sharing my gifts, taking a stand on some important matter, or offering a small act of kindness to others. I hope to broadcast seeds of kindness far and wide, trusting some greater power helps each one find a fertile place on this earth, somewhere I could never have imagined. I will pray that forces greater than my own will protect that seed and nurture it as it grows into something beyond my wildest dreams.

Chapter Twenty-Six

No Hard Feelings

My friend John Maxwell was a complex man who thrived on solving complicated problems. But he left us with the simplest of gifts: a song to sing at his memorial celebration containing words to remember him by.

John passed away unexpectedly on March 9, 2018. Later that evening, I sat down to watch the Pixar movie *Coco*, something that had been on my to-do list for weeks. Set in Mexico, *Coco* is the story of Miguel, a twelve-year-old boy whose love for music (something forbidden by his family for mysterious reasons) sets him on a journey into the Land of the Dead, a place where souls worry that they will disappear completely if they are forgotten by those still living. *Coco* charms while engaging us with serious questions like "What happens after I die?" and "How will I be remembered?" *Coco* also affirms the power music possesses to bind us together in community across generations and worlds.

Music was the starting point for my friendship with John and its sustaining force over fifteen years. We played together in multiple ensembles, where he handled keyboard, vocals, and guitar. For six years we were both members (along with Kim, Jack, and Jim) of what we called the Celtic Band, which provided instrumental accompaniment at worship services every couple of months at the church we attended. John's talent shined brightest when playing melody lines on the recorder. On one occasion with our Celtic Band, he married whimsy and genius by playing both his soprano and alto recorders at the same time, creating a beautiful chord that complemented our sound. John was one of the few people I know who could conceptualize that idea and then execute it to perfection.

But complications following neck surgery left him with hands abandoned by their arms—suddenly and unfairly—robbing them of their mobility and strength to make music. I recall visiting John a few months following his surgery. After we chatted for a few minutes, I joked that we would need to find him an instrument he could play that required only his feet, to which he replied, "Let me show you what I am doing on the piano." He sat at his piano bench, a stack of books on each side upon which he rested his elbows, and proceeded to play a five-finger melody with his right hand, accompanied by a single bass note with the left. It was a simple tune that offered testimony that *defeat* is not a word found in the language of music. I left him that day comforted to know he was in good company—with music of his own making.

A month or so later, his Celtic bandmates brainstormed what instrument John might be able to play given the physical limits now imposed upon him. We purchased a set of harmonicas and a neck holder under the assumption that it would allow John to access the instrument with minimal help from his arms.

But there was a problem: the damage to John's arms prevented him from moving the harmonica from side to side to produce different notes. Embracing this as just another problem to be solved using his creativity and tools, John attached the harmonica holder that wraps around one's neck to a block of wood with a hole bored in the bottom. The block was then placed on a microphone stand, which he could hold with both hands hanging near his waist. By shifting the stand back and forth, John was able to find the targeted note in the harmonica's mouthpiece. We were all amazed (but not surprised) at how quickly he developed into a very good harmonica player. Practicing harmonica and walks around his neighborhood became key therapeutic activities on John's earthly journey toward healing.

Within a few months, John was back with the Celtic Band as we provided instrumental accompaniment for occasional Sunday-morning worship services at our church. When we gathered for our biweekly practices, I was impressed by the way John handled his misfortune with a positive attitude. He never complained, calling his ailment the "Thing That Happened." I would have been angered by the inability of medical experts to chart a path toward full recovery, but John reframed his experience as an "opportunity" and "impetus for discovery."

Shortly before his death, John began sharing the Avett Brothers song "No Hard Feelings" with friends. In a message to his friend Bill, John wrote, "Here is a song I like a lot, which I thought you might enjoy if you have not heard it already. I am also including the lyrics so that you can follow along if you like. Have fun."

A couple of weeks later, John was gone.

***

The four remaining members of the Celtic Band were invited by John's wife and daughter to play at the open house celebrating John's life, held at their home on Saint Patrick's Day. Our plan was to offer instrumental tunes from the Celtic, Taize, and rock and roll genres, which we had played with him. At the request of his wife, we would also perform John's latest song discovery.

When we practiced "No Hard Feelings" a couple of nights before the occasion, I wondered if John had sensed his time was short. The song's opening line poses a question we tend to ignore as we move through each day, but one which John had likely considered often over the prior two years: Will I be ready for death when the time comes?

At the open house event honoring John, the Celtic Band assembled midafternoon on a wooden deck in the backyard in front of dozens of friends and family as they mingled over potluck recipes and an array of beverage options. After breezing through the first ten songs on our list, the time arrived to close out the memorial concert with John's newest favorite song, Kim singing lead vocals and me providing harmony. Perhaps because we knew the weightiness of the lyrics ahead, we struggled to find our rhythm early in the song. We found our groove as we reached the final chorus, which ends with a line that is repeated four times, each one quieter than the prior, the last in a whisper, more spoken than sung. It contained a statement from John that he left this life without any enemies. His message drifted over the backyard and hung in the air, leaving many of us to wonder about our ability to make the same claim.

When our song tribute was over and we had packed up our instruments, I ran into Amy, who had performed in bands with us over the years. (John loved her voice.) "Did you see the robin?" she asked. "It landed in the pecan tree behind you guys just as you started that last song. It hopped around from branch to branch, and when the song was over, it flew away."

Others reported seeing that solitary American robin take in our final song that afternoon. Perhaps it was just passing through, seeking shelter from the light drizzle that arrived as we began that final song. But I have no doubt that the visitor was our friend John, or at least his inimitable spirit. How could it not be? The American robin would be his vessel of choice, a symbol of hope as spring appears and the cold and dark days of winter pass. It possesses a whistling voice using rapid pitch changes a recorder player would appreciate. Its song follows a regular rhythm and forms a message John may have wanted us to hear as we struggled with his loss: "Cheerily, cheer up, cheer up, cheerily, cheer up."[1]

I am confident John was pleased with the sight from his perch, his friends and family sharing memories, the empty chair holding one of his recorders placed next to the band to show that he will always be a part of us. I imagine he felt satisfaction in knowing his directive to hold "no hard feelings" had been seeded in our hearts before he left us and flew away on his journey toward a new home.

***

I find it easy to imagine John today in that transcendent place that is given various names by different faith traditions. Regardless of the word we call it, I expect in "heaven," our souls will be able to recall what we did on this earth, retain the individuality that defined us here, remember those we loved, and hope to not be forgotten. For John, a man who left this earth believing he had no enemies, I imagine it to be a place where he can make new friends.

I picture John in the company of two gentlemen who left this world a couple of days after him. One is Nokie Edwards, whose electric guitar work as a member of the instrumental group the Ventures (best known for their hits "Walk, Don't Run" and the theme song to *Hawaii Five-0*) helped to define the "surf-rock" sound popular in the 1960s. (We played one of their compositions, "Apache," at John's memorial.) Edwards died on March 12 due to a recurring infection following hip surgery three months earlier. The other is Stephen Hawking, theoretical physicist, cosmologist, and author who suffered from amyotrophic lateral sclerosis (ALS or Lou Gehrig's disease) that paralyzed him for decades. Despite losing his speech, he was still able to work, communicating through a speech-generating device by using a single cheek muscle. Hawking died on March 14, five days after John.

I picture the three walking together in a new neighborhood, freed from bodies that limited them on earth. John is between his famous friends, his spirit doing what it did here on this earth—connecting technical and creative worlds and, in the process, bringing diverse individuals together in community. I hear John translating the technical jargon of theoretical physics into a language a guitar player can understand, explaining the mathematics underlying the melody and pulse of rock music to the musician. I see him describing to Hawking the power music possesses to heal that goes far beyond what could ever be explained by science. And he tells them both about the peace that comes from being able to reflect on a life well lived and from knowing he will never be forgotten by those who loved him because he left them something to remember.

***

In the climactic scene in the movie *Coco*, Miguel brings his grandfather's song back from the Land of the Dead and sings it to his family. The song restores memories of loved ones who are now gone and moves the family to accept music back into their lives. "Remember Me" (which won the 2017 Academy Award for Best Original Song) expresses a universal wish to not be forgotten after we are gone.

Regardless of your concept of afterlife, the desire to be remembered burns within each of us. For those we leave behind, they can be comforted by remembering the loved ones they have lost. So the real question is: Will you *leave something to remember* to make that wish come true? Will it be your welcoming smile, or your joyous laughter? A treasured family recipe, or the heirloom china on which to serve it? The walls you erected to separate us, or the bridges you built to bring people together? The time you spent listening to someone share their story, or a story you shared? Or perhaps a simple song you wanted friends to sing containing parting words to keep in their hearts?

The answer is up to me . . . to you . . . to us all.

---

[1] "American Robin Sounds," All About Birds, Cornell Lab, accessed May 18, 2023, https://www.allaboutbirds.org/guide/American_Robin/sounds#.

Chapter Twenty-Seven

Finding a Blessing

Even when silent, it commanded full attention. The simple act of strapping it to my belt raised my anxiety level. I learned from experience it might vibrate at any moment and a cryptic message would appear on its tiny screen. I never liked the pager, but I accepted the fact that the work couldn't be done without it.

I had signed up for an on-call assignment to be the only chaplain at this major trauma center from five o'clock in the afternoon until eight the next morning. I had been blessed with a quiet evening, so around 9:30 p.m., I decided to lie down on the pullout futon couch in the pastoral care office. If the past eight months had taught me anything, it was that sleep can be elusive when covering "the big house" alone.

I wasn't the only one anticipating a sleepless night. A nurse from the seventh floor called saying a mother wanted to meet a chaplain in the chapel. I told the nurse I would wait for her outside its entrance on the lower level.

There were no visitors there at this late hour, only a pair of janitors holding the reins of whirring machines designed to clean and polish the floor to a sanitized shimmer and shine. They ignored me as I stood in silence, anticipating the upcoming conversation. The request to meet in the chapel was unusual, I thought, hoping it signaled she was a woman of faith and our discussion might be a bit easier to navigate.

Within a few minutes, a small Hispanic woman appeared from the elevator bank to my right. Tears filled her reddened eyes. After we exchanged greetings, I opened the chapel door and gestured for her to enter ahead of me. She paused inside to scan the room before selecting a front-row pew. I sat down beside her, and she immediately shifted away, a move that distanced us by only a couple of feet but, at the same time, created an immense emotional gulf between us.

I asked her what I could do to help her. She stared ahead and began to share her story in fragments. Her sister had recently passed away, and she was still mourning that loss. Her two-year-old son now lay upstairs connected to a respirator. She felt lost, with no place to turn. "That's why I asked to see you. I am looking for an answer to just one question," she said, turning to look at me. "What must I do so God will make all of this go away?"

I had no idea what to say. Lacking an answer, I asked the woman about her son, her sister, her family, her current emotions. I inquired about her faith experience and her supporting relationships. She told me she had not been raised in the church and had no system of religious belief.

"That is why I am here," she said. "Tell me—what must I do to make this all go away?"

I told the woman she was not alone, that in the hospital, everyone from chaplains to those of little faith sought an answer to the question, "Where is God in all of this?" But her tears continued to flow, and she returned to the same question: "You are a pastor, so you must have the answer. What must I do to make this go away?"

I felt like correcting her by saying, "I am not a pastor, only a naive layperson trying to help others through this eight-month volunteer assignment." But I knew that description was no longer accurate and not at all helpful. I suggested that she would need to find the answer herself, that this would involve a journey, one that I would help her along the way if she liked. Her chin dropped down to her chest.

I tried to ignore a sinking feeling deep inside. I was seated next to a mother who was asking the most profound of questions: Why would a benevolent God visit pain and suffering on the most innocent among us? But I offered no answers, only asked smaller questions.

I tried to coax her into sharing more about her family, but every avenue I explored became a blind alley that seemed to make matters worse. When I asked about the small necklace she wore, she told me it was a gift from her sister and that it reminded her of how they'd fought shortly before her death.

"I am sorry" was the only response I could find.

After we talked another twenty minutes or so and the time felt right, I prayed that God would help her find meaning in all that was happening to her and her family. I then escorted her to her son's room, where we stood by his bed as he lay in the peaceful stillness of the darkened room. Tears remained in her weary eyes as I left.

I doubt either of us got much sleep that night.

***

Three days later I returned to the hospital on a Sunday afternoon to begin my final on-call assignment as chaplain. I tried to find positive energy from knowing that my eight-month odyssey through the clinical pastoral education program would come to an end seven hours later and I would hand off the pager to another chaplain for the last time.

I prayed for a quiet shift that might free up time to look for the woman I'd spoken with in the chapel three nights earlier. Memories of our encounter had visited me often since that night, and I wondered how she and her son might be doing. But within seconds after the pager hit my hand, it began to vibrate. A nurse on the fifth floor was requesting a chaplain.

When I arrived, she pointed to a couple occupying a small alcove in the corner. "Their son is being moved to the ICU this afternoon," she told me. "They do not speak English, only Spanish. They are very upset."

The father was seated while his wife paced the adjacent hall, talking on her cell phone in her native language. I knew enough Spanish to make small talk with the father, but I recognized that this conversation demanded a level of clarity that stretched far beyond my ability. I asked the nurse to request one of the hospital's translators to help. Since it was Sunday and there was no translator on the premises, we would be connected via phone with a translator to help us with our discussion.

A nurse set a landline speakerphone on a small table between our chairs. With the help of the translator, I introduced myself to the father and asked about his son. He told me the teenager's condition was getting worse. I followed up with more questions to explore how the father was feeling, but his shoulders drooped, his answers became terse, and his face grew sullen, bordering on anger.

His growing frustration with the clumsiness of our translated conversation reminded me of how ineffective I had felt during the late-night discussion with the mother three nights before. Again, I was fumbling and failing to find a way to connect with a person I had been called on to comfort.

As I considered what I might do to try to improve the dynamics of our conversation, I recalled advice I had received near the start of my chaplaincy experience: "Families are your best source for finding out what they need." In an act that might be described as informed desperation to salvage something from our visit, I landed on the only thing left worth trying. More a plea than a question, I said to the translator, "Please, ask him if there is anything, anything at all, I can do right now that would be helpful for him and his family."

The father sat upright as he looked my way for the first time in minutes. His response was immediate and clear. "I would like a priest to offer a blessing on my son."

I now knew what to do. I remembered the sign posted outside the hospital chapel indicating a Spanish-language mass was held there every Sunday afternoon. I could not recall the exact time of the service, but I excused myself and jolted down the hall to the elevator that would take me to the lower level. When I opened the door, there stood a priest conducting mass in Spanish to the largest crowd I had ever seen worship in this space. My silent prayer had been answered.

I stood in the back of the chapel as attendees moved forward to accept the elements of the Holy Eucharist. I worshipped with them as best I could, but my thoughts drifted toward what I might say to convince this priest to follow me to visit the boy and his parents.

When the service ended, most worshippers headed toward the exit while a few others moved forward to help the priest return the chalice, paten, candles, and linens to a small storage closet to the side of the chapel. I inched forward, waiting for the crowd to thin and clear the way for me to approach the priest. When I was within five feet of him, a short woman turned to face me and smiled. It took a moment for me to recognize her as the troubled woman I had sat with in this same chapel three nights before.

"How are you?" I asked.

"Better. Much better," she said. "Thank you."

I wanted to find out what had happened since our talk, but I was on a new mission to assist a troubled father who I feared might be thinking I had deserted him.

I stepped up to the padre, a short bespectacled man in his sixties or seventies, and said, "Excuse me, Father. I am the chaplain on call. There is a teenage boy who is a patient on the fifth floor. The family only speaks Spanish, and the parents have asked if it would be possible for you to bless their son."

"I know that child and his family," he replied with youthful enthusiasm. "Let us go to them at once."

Moments later, I stood toward the side of the room as the priest and parents exchanged greetings and positioned themselves around the child's bed. The priest consoled the parents in language they understood, using words of comfort they needed to hear. As he performed the Catholic sacrament of Anointing of the Sick, the face of the boy's father was transformed from an expression of deep despair into one of abundant hope.

＊

Over the next few months, I tried to unpack the meaning of these final two experiences as chaplain. Despite my self-perceived inadequacies in the role, I found comfort in the lasting mental image of these separate incidents where a mother and a father found something helpful from our visits. I know I deserve none of the credit because, in both cases, some greater power was at work inside these hospital walls. God was present through the conversations, the awkward silences, the questions asked, the quest to find a priest, my reencounter with the young mother.

It would be easy to explain it all as fate, chance, coincidence, or some other word that speaks to the randomness of events. Instead, the unexpected outcome moved me to *believe in providence*—God's extraordinary, benevolent, and timely intervention. It was through his or her omniscient power that I was able to honor a father's request for a blessing and, in the process, receive the blessing I needed to bring closure to my clinical chaplain experience. The father's blessing came in the form of a priest able to offer a meaningful sacrament to his son, while mine

arrived in the form of a broad smile of gratitude from a woman I feared I had failed.

Chapter Twenty-Eight

The First Day of Fall

Her voice message was brief and to the point. "Dad went to be with the Lord." Seven simple words, plus a couple of more I could not decipher as Mom choked out the news through her grief.

It was the first day of fall (September 23, 2019), and the world felt like a smaller place because a beloved husband, father, friend, farmer, and World War II veteran finally got an answer to a request that bore witness to his deep faith. "Pastor, don't pray for me to get well," he had said. "Pray for me to be able to go see my Lord." Ralph Dykstra left those who loved him with memories of a gentle man and feeling a different type of pain than the physical kind he had endured with grace during his last few years here on earth.

I hadn't marked the first day of fall on my calendar. But I sensed it approaching. The days were growing shorter. Shadows lengthened as the sun sank lower in the sky. Creatures were taking flight in search of new homes. When that day finally arrived, it brought with it my first tears and immeasurable gratitude for having him as my father, teacher, and role model of how to close out a life well lived.

Dad taught me more than most of my professors in college and graduate school—the practical kind of knowledge that good parents understand is important to pass on to the next generation. He showed me how to throw a baseball, how to hammer a nail into a board straight and true, and how to fix it when I failed and it bent. He demonstrated how important it was to "measure twice and cut once," not just as it related to carpentry but as a metaphor for how to approach key decisions with deliberation and accuracy.

Dad also taught me how to drive the 1965 Ford F-100 pickup my brother, Curt, nicknamed the Aqua Runner due to its greenish-blue exterior, powerful 352 CI engine, and responsive manual three-speed transmission. My lesson came more in the form of a challenge than instruction. "Drive it up to the house," he told me as we stood in the middle of our gladiolus field. I imagine he got a few chuckles out of the starts and stalls that ensued. But I made it to my destination, and at the age of fourteen, I learned how to drive a stick shift, and no one got hurt in the process. It was just one example of the way he prepared me to go out into the world and take on whatever obstacles came my way.

Dad valued consistency and uniformity. This was apparent in the balanced landscape design of the evergreens he planted around his house and regularly trimmed to level perfection. It was visible in the laser-straight rows of corn he planted in an era long before GPS-based farming was imagined—something not easy in an era of two-row planting equipment because any error made in one pass through the field would be compounded with the next one.

This was a feat his father-in-law found impossible to achieve given his tendency to become distracted behind the wheel of his tractor, resulting in fields that more resembled Lombard Street in San Francisco than Interstate 80 as it follows its linear path from Chicago to Denver. One spring, Dad volunteered to plant Grandpa Ahrens' soybean field for him. After he completed the job and they surveyed the finished field of straight and perfectly spaced rows, Grandpa commented, "You know, you get more beans in a crooked row."

I doubt that Dad ever bought into the unconventional "wisdom" of my grandfather's quip, because steadiness was imbedded into his essence. It was reflected not just in the planting but in how he operated as a straight shooter in all his business dealings. Members of the management team at the factory where he worked for nearly thirty years were known to seek him out when looking for perspective, confident that Ralph Dykstra would give them the unvarnished truth, no doubt because he never shied from sharing it countless times when they hadn't asked.

My dad walked an orderly path through a life that brought him more than his fair share of twists and turns. This was most evident following his second stroke. It was during these final six years of his life, when I saw him less and admired him more, that Dad offered an outward portrayal of inner strength. He remained resilient even though he was sidelined from the outdoor tasks he loved, found it increasingly difficult to navigate around his home, and suffered through dimming eyesight that made reading a challenge. "Sometimes a person can live too long" was the closest thing to a grievance I heard him utter.

In fact, I don't recall him *ever* complaining! During the six months when I worked with him on the memoir covering his World War II experiences, I learned more about his early childhood. As a novice writer, I knew enough about how to construct an engaging narrative to be dangerous, so I started looking for the personal conflict that drove the protagonist, my dad, to a critical decision that would test and reframe his character. In hindsight, I wonder why I felt the need to find a personal conflict in a story that revolved around the violence and tragedy of the most damaging war this earth has seen.

After a few discussions, I identified a promising candidate for an inciting incident in Dad's adolescent years. He had grown up in an era when children, particularly males, were valued for their role as "free" farm labor. His father (whom he called "Pa") owned a thousand laying hens at the time, and the daily tasks of grinding the feed, changing the bedding straw, and picking the eggs had all been done by hand. At the age of fourteen, my Dad had been tasked with handling all these chores, a responsibility he had continued to bear for six years until he had enlisted in the military a few months before his twentieth birthday.[1]

So I began to imagine a compelling narrative about my father's situation that went like this:

Our hero longs to serve his country but is forced to stay at home because there is no one else to take care of the farm. He is too young to enlist on his own, and despite his repeated pleas, his father refuses to sign the papers allowing him to join the military. Our hero feels torn between opposing forces and faces a powerful dilemma that must be resolved: Which is more important? Dedication to one's family? Or allegiance to one's country? The conflict culminates in a scene where the son's resentment at being trapped at home reaches a boiling point. He confronts his father, asking him, arguing with him, demanding his release.

"That's a great storyline," I thought to myself.

With this potential storyline in mind, I would push Dad to share his frustration with the situation during our weekly conversations regarding the memoir. I would offer leading comments like "I bet that was pretty hard on you" or "Weren't you upset that you were forced to stay home?" Finally, after multiple probes like these on my part, he called a halt to my narrative nonsense by stating the simple truth of the situation, "I was the oldest son at home. Pa needed help with this chicken farm, so that's what I did."[2]

The "author" in me had hoped Dad would grumble and gripe about the raw deal birth timing had levied on him. But he refused to go there. In the process of discovering the "story" I was looking for was not true, I was given another useful lesson from my father—the value of accepting whatever situation life throws at you and doing what is demanded of you with steadfast grace.

After a third stroke brought him to the hospital, the chronic nerve pain that had been his constant companion took on a greater intensity. During his final two months with us, as his earthly struggle reached its final rounds, Dad stayed in character. He remained polite to all his caregivers. He accepted guests and engaged them in conversation as best he could. He recited poems lodged deep in his memory to the nurses who tended to him. Even though his physical therapists told him, "I don't think this is going to do much good," Dad continued to be a "good soldier" as he expended his limited energy against each task they asked him to perform. He was able to cut through the fog of his own pain to ask about his grandchildren and great-grandchildren. He remained the protector, looking out for the welfare of his wife of seventy-two years. He was a gentleman, a gentle man, to the end.

But most impressive, in his final days Dad demonstrated an unwavering belief in a life after this one. "How does that hymn go?" he asked rhetorically one day toward the end. "There'll be no sorrow there. No more burdens to bear. No more sickness, no pain."[3] His approaching death galvanized his faith and offered powerful testimony to his belief in Jesus's promise to him of an abundant life after this one.

In my brother's beautiful reflection read at Dad's funeral, one line reached into me and grabbed my full attention: "He made growing up easy and hard at the same time." I never asked Curt what he meant by that sentence because I understood in my own way that it was true. Dad didn't preach to me about right and wrong. He demonstrated it in his actions. He didn't shower me with praise, but I always knew he believed in me. He didn't make a big show of his love for his wife, children, grandchildren, great-grandchildren. He expressed it through the sparkle in his eyes when we were with him.

In his book *The Second Mountain*, best-selling author David Brooks defines one's legacy as the system of belief and behavior that endures long after they are gone, something he calls a *moral ecology*. Brooks could have easily been describing my dad, a man whose life served as a reminder for us all to *live your legacy*.

Now that my father is gone, I am different in ways I do not yet completely understand. But I know one thing for certain: today I now more fully appreciate how the ninety-six years represented by a hyphen between the 1923 and 2019 etched on Dad's headstone defined a moral ecology that will live inside me forever.

***

The farmer ethos ingrained in Dad might have appreciated the timing of his own death on the first day of fall. Autumn is the season when the toil and hardships experienced during the preceding ones reach an end, the fruits of all labors are gathered, and the yield is measured and counted. I find comfort in knowing that although his earthly life is complete, Dad lives on in eternity because that is what he believed.

I see autumn in a new way now, not as the time to mourn the passing of summer but as the onset of the most beautiful season of the year. This fall, and I suspect every year ahead, I will take in the changes this season brings with renewed appreciation. I'll watch as the leaves wither and fade, letting go of their beautiful time with us, paving the way for new life ahead. They will find their rest on the ground around me. I'll see them blow about like freed spirits carried by silent forces. In them, I will sense that my father is nearby yet far away, experiencing a new life I can never fully understand . . . a glorious life after death . . . a death that took him away from me on the first day of fall.

***

A couple of weeks after I completed this chapter, Sandy opened her Bible, and a small card fell out. Inside was a brief thank-you note Dad had written to me three years before his death, which closed with these words:

Read Micah chapter 6, verses 6–9. Verse 8 is a guide to live one's life by.

"What does the Lord require of you but to do justice, and to love kindness,

and to walk humbly with your God?"

Upon rereading that scripture, I marveled at the degree to which Dad had lived out his life true to that instruction to me. That single verse from a minor Old Testament prophet said with succinct clarity what had taken me over two thousand words to describe.

---

[1] My mom later told me that Dad shared with her the fact that he had missed the first two months of eighth grade because his father (a member of the local school board) had made him work on the farm instead. If not for an early freeze that fall, Dad was not sure when he would have been able to return to school.

[2] Ralph Dykstra, *In the Service of My Country: I Never Regretted a Day*, ed. Larry V. Dykstra (Dallas: Inspired Forever Books, 2016), 8.

[3] The name of the hymn is "What a Day that Will Be."

Chapter Twenty-Nine

Confessions of a Truant Servant

Our discussion leader asked an insightful question, a version of which I had considered hundreds of times after my visits to the rooms of severely ill children and their caregivers: In our service to others, how do we know if we really made a difference?

I had been visiting children's hospitals for the past ten years, where I delivered live music that provided encouragement and comfort in a place where children suffered and parents worried. I captured some of the more amazing responses in my book titled *Musical Hugs: Succeeding Through Serving, One Song at a Time*:

- The time I noticed a ten-year-old boy who seemed not at all interested in me or my song tapping his foot beneath the sheet in perfect time with the music, demonstrating the irresistible power of music.

- How the quiet ballad I played to an anxious toddler distracted him so well that a nurse was able to give him a shot he never saw coming or felt.

- An act of caring by the mother of a patient when she suggested I visit the boy next door because he received no visitors.

- The way a little girl engaged in "This Little Light of Mine" as her father and I sang to her a couple of days after she emerged from a lengthy coma.

- And much, much more.

I recognized it was unreasonable to expect to witness the amazing healing power of music at every visit, but I always hoped that something positive would happen. But more often than I cared to accept, I left uncertain about whether my visit had made an impact. Once I left someone's room after sharing a song, I was not privy to what followed. While I tried to convince myself that something good came from each visit, it became easy to wonder if a song or two from a stranger made any difference.

Over time, I started to find this absence of positive feedback more difficult to accept. On some days, I needed to combat the headwinds of doubt that produced an inner resistance to going to the hospital. Since the service I offered was not essential to the medical care for these severely ill children, it became easier to think that my music would not be missed. Servant truancy crept in as an acceptable option.

On the days I went to the hospital, I felt tempted to skip one of the floors or rooms where the child life specialists suggested a kiddo might benefit from my short visit and a song. I developed an effective counterargument to offset my hesitation: Denying a child the offer of a song was not my decision to make because something unexpected and wonderful may have resulted from that visit. This reasoning usually worked.

So when the question of "How do we know we had any impact?" was raised at the workshop I was attending, it felt like a familiar one that went to the crux of my lingering efficacy concerns about this tricky business of serving others. I had no intention of expressing my self-doubts in front of friends until one of them suggested I might have some useful perspective to share since *Musical Hugs* had recently been released.

I did my best to mask my lack of confidence by explaining to the forty or so adults present how I talked myself into trusting that something positive came from my musical rounds. I noted that on those occasions where I was certain there was no impact, I forced myself to focus on the next visit, not the last one. I treated it like a baseball pitcher who gave up a home run or a quarterback who tossed an interception: forget the event in order to make the next throw with confidence. My purpose in doing so was not to ignore what had taken place but to set it aside so I wouldn't be bringing any lingering self-doubt into the next room.

My comments seemed to satisfy most of those attending the session. But then Martha stood and offered a view from the other side of the song. She shared the story of her nine-year-old son's recovery from multiple complex facial-cranial surgeries. When he was four, following the sixth of thirteen painful procedures, Tim's head and eyes had been bandaged and swollen. Unable to see, Tim had required the comfort that only comes from feeling someone was always by his side. The presence of his parents was the only thing that helped ease his pain and anxiety, which must have been immense.

Martha shared that on the third day after that surgery, my friends and therapeutic music mentors Jim Newton and Paul G. Hill of KidLinks[1] arrived in Tim's room and provided music for him. In the middle of one song, Tim let go of his mother's hand. Martha described how the music had offered Tim emotional support in a new and compelling way. Music touches us all, but on that day a song offered a healing touch of its own—consoling a little boy, telling him he was safe and secure in the world of caring that surrounded him.

I imagine Jim and Paul may have noticed as Tim moved his hand away from his mother's during their song, but there was no way for them to understand its significance. How could they? Our service of therapeutic music arrives out of context and at unexpected moments. Our music is shared and experienced in real time, with no sense for the before or after.

Martha's perspective suggested signs of the healing power of music are presented to me all the time but may appear in the form of responses I am unable to interpret. Tim's act of moving his hand away from his mother's was nothing noteworthy to a visitor, but for Martha, who had been by her son's side for days, it was a significant moment made possible by the power of a single song. Her comments changed me. I stopped playing the role of truant servant and returned to the hospital playing my guitar.

I will confess my sin of servant truancy in terms of both thought and deed. I see now I became too absorbed in my own self-doubts to realize something positive always results from service for both the giver and the receiver. If I am to be genuine in my intent to serve others, I shouldn't need to have people tell me to know I am doing the right thing. More specifically, Martha helped me realize I shouldn't need to witness the healing power of music every time to believe something good comes from each "musical hug" I share. Now I know I need to have faith and believe in things not seen because even though I may not see it with my own eyes, my God does.

---

[1] For more information about KidLinks, visit www.kidlinks.org.

Chapter Thirty

The Fingers of God

The pastor's words rang true for me that morning:

> *Every once in a while—and never on demand—you get an epiphany, a gift of being in the right place at the right time when the veil between heaven and earth is so thin you experience a fullness of life you usually miss. You sense the presence of God and angels; and it both delights and scares the bejesus out of you.*[1]

Scary might be a good word to summarize my time as chaplain for eight months at a large metropolitan children's hospital. To be sure, many of my experiences there brought me to the thinnest of places. The hospitalization of a child can bring parents, family, and caregivers alike to their existential limits. Even those of little faith begin a desperate search for help from some higher power, seeking to find an answer to the question chaplains are trained to consider: Where is God in all of this?

A more tranquil encounter with a "thin place" happened on the twenty-fifth day of my pilgrimage on the Camino de Santiago, crossing northern Spain. Outside the town of Triacastela, the Camino divides into two routes before they reunite ten to fifteen kilometers ahead, depending on which road you take. I chose the one less traveled. Although it required a more strenuous climb, it was the shorter of the two options.

I walked alone throughout the chilly morning, catching an occasional glimpse of a pilgrim or two ahead in the distance. After a long gradual ascent, I found myself on an empty road high above a green and verdant valley on my left. The clouds were hovering so low over my head I felt the need to duck at times. Here, the veil that divides this world from the one beyond seemed to disappear. I sensed I was no longer walking alone but in the company of the Divine. All of my being was seized by the ethereal quality of the moment.

Throughout my entire 450-mile walk on the Camino, I felt that God was nearby. But the feeling on this day was different, not because his or her presence was stronger but because I was more open to receiving it. In this thin place I knew there was "something bigger" yet formless surrounding me—above, below, beside, inside. Here, I felt smaller yet safe. I became aware of my insignificance.

I found my words were insufficient to describe this experience. Have you ever tried to describe the expansive beauty of the Grand Canyon to someone? Or express the deep joy and thanksgiving you felt holding a newborn child, maybe your own, moments after its birth? In scenes like these, experience outruns the ability of our language to express it. You could pause and take a picture, but chances are you will receive a far greater blessing by *living in the moment* than by spending time trying to *capture that moment* on film.

***

The origins of the term *thin place* trace back to the Celtic tradition, no doubt inspired by the stunning beauty of windswept places such as the Isle of Iona and the Slieve League Cliffs of Donegal. The commercial value of a thin-place experience is evident in the number of travel agencies offering pricey tours that bring guests to ancient, sacred sites in Ireland and Scotland to explore the mystical history, myths, and spirituality associated with them.

I doubt thin places exist only in well-defined geographical locations; nor do I think you need to book a tour or spend days walking an ancient pilgrimage route to find one. I suspect they are all around us, waiting to be found. All we need to do is take the time to slow down, pay attention, and open ourselves to discovery.

I have discovered a thin place in the sanctuary of First Presbyterian Church Dallas, which I have regularly attended for the past twenty-plus years. The structure was built in the Greek Revival–style architecture in 1912 and holds a rich history. On many Sunday mornings, between the time I spend with the children's choir during Sunday school hour and the 11:00 a.m. worship service, I will sneak into this space built for communal worship and find myself alone. I take a seat in one of the pews toward the side of the fan-shaped sanctuary, a design that allows for a surprising sense of intimacy and connection despite the expansiveness of the room.

First, I will look toward the gilded Celtic cross, which dominates the wall behind the chancel, framed by the cylindrical organ pipes that border and ascend on each side. My gaze will shift to the large stained-glass window on the wall to the right memorializing members of the 150-plus-year-old congregation. I will take in the large image of Jesus in the center panel, cradling a lost sheep in his arms.

But inevitably, I will lift my eyes upward toward the vaulted ceiling and the great glass dome that hovers overhead. I will follow the Greek fret design that establishes the outermost ring, admire the sixteen sections of art glass supported by copper ribs, and try to count the repeated pairs of bronze-and-gold art glass rings that grow smaller as they approach the eye of the dome (the oculus) in the center. In its entirety, this dome is a masterpiece, an artistic partnership of glass and metal working together to create a sight that impresses at first glance yet requires time to study and appreciate in its fullest.

But the dome becomes transcendent when an unexpected element animates it and converts it into a thin place for me. For a few weeks each spring and fall, the trajectory of the Dallas sun sinks a bit lower in the sky, and a new feature appears. On those mornings, rays of sunlight sneak through the arches of the structure that surround and protect the inner dome, creating the appearance of what I imagine to be God's five fingers placed upon me and my people, a visible reminder that he or she covers and protects us all.[2] In the solitude of that moment, in that familiar space, I sense the presence of God above me, our shepherd Jesus standing beside me, the Holy Spirit all around me—and I am blessed with a sense of comfort that remains with me as I go out into the world during the following week.

***

You might be wondering how it is possible to *find thin places* of your own if these are, as usually described, spontaneous and unexpected experiences that take us by surprise. But I believe they are accessible once we overcome our numbness to the world around us that results from eating the same thing for breakfast, driving the same route to work each day, and sleeping on the same side of the bed every night.

Here's a simple remedy. Take a journey into the creation that surrounds you. Allow yourself to be touched by what you see, smell, and hear. Find a spot where you can lie in the grass. Close your eyes, and listen to your soul, that quiet voice that gets drowned out by the daily grind. Ask all your senses to do the work they were designed to do. Think of a lost loved one. Consider where they are—far away yet nearby because you remember them in this moment. Imagine them smiling at you. Feel the closeness of God surrounding you in this moment. Thank that transcendent power for letting you dwell in this thin place. And know that once you allow yourself to be touched by that "something bigger," it will remain a part of you forever.

---

[1] George A. Mason, "Holy, Holey, Wholly" (Sermon), Wilshire Baptist Church, Dallas, February 10, 2019.
[2] I first heard this description from Sarah Werner, a child of our church who gave a homily on Youth Sunday during her senior year in high school.

Chapter Thirty-One

Theology of the Journey

"Your theology . . . I found it hard to relate to," said my colleague Matt in what I knew from experience was merely the headline for a blistering critique to follow.

He was referring to the paper I had written as the final assignment for our clinical pastoral education program. The seven of us who had made it through the eight-month program were required to share our personal theologies, which had no doubt been reshaped by serving as chaplains in a large metropolitan children's hospital. I had titled mine *Walking Beside Others: A Theology of the Journey*, where I used my recent trek on the Camino de Santiago in Spain as a metaphor for my pilgrimage through the pastoral care world. The paper touched on common themes such as learning to bear our burdens, accepting the challenges we face, and getting in touch with "something bigger."

Matt's opening salvo was the first time I had been directly challenged about my understanding of my relationship with God. "There must be something I can say in response to this," I thought to myself. Perhaps something like "It's not like I worship pagan gods, nor do I steal from the piggy banks of little children. I am a good person in God's eyes . . . I think."

Following a kinder comment by another colleague, Matt caught his second wind and continued his critical examination. "I mean, you wrote about journeys but failed to express any firm beliefs. It seems you have no North Star to guide you. Without a belief system, you could easily get unmoored in the face of life's challenges."

Too deep in thought and too slow to respond, I saw my chance for rebuttal disappear when our supervisor announced it was time to discuss Shannon's theology paper. We had learned that her stepdaughter had been killed during Lenten season a couple of years earlier. She had shared only a few details of the tragedy, the outcome of a botched robbery at the fast-food restaurant where the eighteen-year-old had worked, so none of us knew what to expect on this first Monday after Easter.

"I am so glad Easter has finally come and gone," Shannon said softly as she stared down at the floor. "Yesterday was the day when Christians all over the world celebrated their belief that Jesus was raised from the dead." After a brief pause, she looked up, cleared her throat, and declared, "I am glad Jesus came back to life because, if I had my way, I would hang his sorry ass right back on that cross!"

I recall wondering if she could say this and not get smitten on the spot. Apparently, she could, because Shannon was still with us, raging on. "God may have saved his son, Jesus, but he did nothing to save our daughter Emily! Where is the justice in that?" Her diatribe against the Almighty was making Jack Nicholson's speech in the climactic scene of *A Few Good Men* seem like a tender reading of a bedtime story to a four-year-old. There was no way to escape her pain.

I found the contrast between the perspectives of my two colleagues both striking and unsettling. In Matt's view, there was no wiggle room. The answers were so clear he questioned why others could not see it that way. He found comfort in his belief that some higher purpose was at work in this hospital where bad things happened to innocent children for no understandable reason. Matt believed his role as chaplain was to deliver that message in the face of suffering.

Shannon was questioning everything. Well, not quite. Her acceptance that God existed was revealed through her anger and pain. She was hell-bent on getting justice, and since God was in control, he or she must be to blame. Bruised and hurting, Shannon didn't want platitudes or Bible verses that may soothe but not solve her pain. God's only son needed to speak to the chaos surrounding her loss. Shannon wanted to "have a little talk with Jesus," although I sensed there was nothing that he could say to her to "make it right." I suspected Matt thought he already knew what Jesus would suggest: that Shannon just needed to be patient because "he'll answer by and by."

Over the next few days, I reread my theology paper many times, scribbling a star next to one passage in particular. When I had first written it, I had thought it was a brilliant use of the Camino metaphor:

The times I felt I came closest to fulfilling the promise inherent in the chaplain title were when I walked beside strangers in their time of greatest need. I comforted them. I offered my hospitality. I mourned with them. I sat beside them in silence because I knew of no words that could provide the answer to the questions reflected in their tears.

After listening to Matt and Shannon, I saw how my theology lacked both clarity and commitment. It rang hollow in contrast to their passionate extremes.

A week later, my "theology of the journey" received a more serious blow in the formal evaluation from my supervisor. While he suggested my "experiential theology" could be a wonderful resource for me, he also wrote:

His continued work will be to name what he brings to his work as chaplain from his Reformed and Presbyterian traditions. Larry knows the language of these traditions well. His ambivalence is about using this language to define who he is as a pastoral care provider.

There it was: ambivalence and all its synonyms staring me in the face. Doubt. Hesitancy. Uncertainty. Irresoluteness. I know the language but resist using it. No mentions of the Divine. No stated beliefs. Only silence in the face of serious questions.

***

I was reared in the Protestant Reformed tradition, where I read the stories from the Bible, memorized the names of all sixty-six books, recited key verses of scripture, learned the Lord's Prayer and Apostle's Creed, tried my best to recall at least two parts of the three-point sermons I sat through each Sunday morning and evening. These were just warm-ups to the main event to gain official church membership—studying the Heidelberg Catechism. Commissioned by a pious German prince in the sixteenth century, it has been the go-to source for learning Calvinist Christian doctrine ever since. The Heidelberg Catechism posed theological questions sixth graders like me were too young and innocent to fathom:

What is your only comfort in life and death?

From where did man's depraved nature come?

What do you understand by the providence of God?

Since Christ died for us, why do we still need to die?

Fortunately, the catechism provided all the answers, although ones written five centuries before I was born. To be accepted as a church member, I needed to recite them with reasonable proximity when asked by stern and stoic Dutch elders. While I was frightened at the time, I now realize these farmers were not going to ask follow-up questions like "What does that mean for you personally?" Their only pedagogical duty was to determine if I had memorized the answers, not to plumb the depths of my understanding.

Matt's harsh assessment revealed that my "theology of the journey" bore no recognizable connection to the faith tradition in which I had been raised. Our supervisor's insight regarding my reticence to use its language offered tangible evidence of a drift away from what I had been taught. Shannon's passionate diatribe toward matters of the Divine exposed my ambivalence. I was left with questions I was not certain how to answer: Had I stopped believing what I had been taught as a child? If so, when had that happened? What did this mean? What did I believe now?

***

These questions bothered me for months that turned into years. I didn't ignore them completely, merely treated them like a nagging toothache that never went away but was not painful enough to warrant a visit to a dentist. I regularly attended worship and Sunday school, which provided insight in the moment but offered little of transforming power. I accepted positions as deacon and elder at my church, although working on matters of church governance did not bring me in closer relationship with God. I even purchased an *Introduction to Theology* book, but less than ten pages into the first chapter, I banished it to a shelf with my other reading rejects. I felt lost, ready to abandon my search for answers.

A breakthrough came when I discovered the work of Barbara Brown Taylor, best-selling author and Episcopal priest whose books offer a personal and candid perspective on matters of faith and spirituality. (She labels herself *spiritual contrarian* on her website. I am not certain what that means, but it sounds cool to me.) Her first memoir, titled *Leaving Church: A Memoir of Faith*, explored the idea that "church" included looking at the Divine from diverse angles. That sounded like useful advice to me.

Early in the book Taylor described a childhood encounter with the Divine Presence outside the walls on any church building. With her powerful sensory vocabulary (using words like *hearing, smelling, floating, pressing down, touching, heating*), Taylor made her experience immediate and real to the reader. Taylor credited her capacity to sense God's presence in nature to the fact that she was not raised in the church so possessed no religious language to describe her experiences.[1] Confident Matt would accuse this leading theological thinker of lacking a "North Star" to guide her beliefs, I felt in good company with her writing.

In my search to hear more of Taylor's ideas, I happened upon an interview titled *Beholding and Believing* that provided me with a distinction that helped me bridge the gap between the religious teachings from my youth and what I had written in my theology paper. According to Taylor, *believing* is about what we learn from others. It is religious teaching about God and the ways we are expected to behave. Here, we are responsible for following an established set of dos and don'ts. In contrast, *beholding* is about engaging in the mysteries of life and paying attention to what we sense, feel, and imagine as a result. It emphasizes the personal encounters with the Divine that force us to reconsider and reshape what we believe. Here, we are responsible for serving what is real. Taylor suggested that embracing both languages can help us make sense out of life.

***

I accepted Taylor's conclusion as an invitation to get back in touch with the believing language I had been taught and reflect on how life experiences had brought personal meaning to the tenets of my faith tradition. As a first step, I returned to the catechism of my youth. I discerned that the Heidelberg Catechism laid out with abundant clarity the key tenets of a faith tradition, which I was able to restate in this manner:

God is above me, looking over me.

Jesus, my Savior, is at my side.

The Holy Spirit surrounds me.

The Bible guides me.

I am called to serve others.

I must treat little children with love, care, and compassion.

I am instructed to care for God's creation.

Heaven awaits me after death.

I was impressed with how the belief system passed down to me had provided a solid foundation within which I could live and grow.

Having reconnected with my "believing" language, I then turned to the "beholding" side of the ledger because I needed to journey into this world and experience pain and love to see God at work in my life. I saw how personal encounters with God's holy presence transformed that belief system into something authentically my own. Through personal encounters with the Divine, my understanding of what it means to be a child of God moved far beyond anything found in the textbook lessons from my youth. For example:

- The lesson that providence is God's almighty and ever-present power was revealed to me when difficult situations were resolved by what felt like an extraordinary and timely intervention by an omniscient power.

- The Bible's promise that Jesus would be my shepherd was fulfilled in the many moments when I felt his guiding and comforting presence walking beside me.

- As a child, I may have sung "His eye is on the sparrow, and I know he watches me," but I felt that promise in "thin places" where I sensed God's holy presence protecting me.

- The Bible's commandment that we "love our neighbor" became real to me when I practiced hospitality and tended to the needs of others.

- While I was taught it is my duty to use my God-given talents for the well-being of others, it was only when I started sharing my music with severely ill children that I felt the spiritual rewards that come from giving of one's self.

- The catechism states we speak of "God as our Father" to remind us to approach prayer with childlike reverence, and the time I spend with little children is what reconnects me to the joy of using one's imagination, something that comes so naturally to them.

- While the first chapter of Genesis tells of how God made heaven and earth, his or her creation fills my senses each time I witness the beauty of a sunset or smell the rich aroma of a newly plowed field.

- The first lesson in the Heidelberg Catechism offers assurance of life everlasting, but these printed words pale in comparison to hearing my father testify to his deep faith shortly before his death by saying, numerous times, "I want to go see my Lord."

Believing and *beholding* both face limits that are addressed by the other. Belief without experience can devolve into unquestioning dogma. Experience without belief may become untethered hedonism. In partnership, belief and experience inform and illuminate each other to bring meaning and understanding to life.

***

If I were to meet Matt and Shannon again, I would thank them for forcing me to reconsider my personal theology, even if it took me far too long to do so. I would tell them that I now embrace a "theology of the journey," albeit a very different one compared to what I wrote a decade ago. It is no longer a passive one where I walk beside others in silence. Rather, it is an active journey that is grounded in beliefs I was taught as a child but avoids holding on to them so tightly that they create a barrier to experiencing God's presence in my life. It requires an openness that allows God to break through the mundane, grab my attention, and surprise and challenge me so I can behold his or her truth for me in the moment. It is a precious journey partnering believing and beholding, bringing me into relationship with God as I travel toward becoming what he or she created me to be.

***

I did not write this chapter to try to convince you to believe as I do. Quite the opposite. I offer it in the spirit of encouragement—that you would follow a similar quest of integrating what you have been taught to believe with what you have experienced in life. But be forewarned: This is difficult and painstaking work. Yet it is worth the effort because by doing so, you may create something worth sharing with others.

---

[1] Barbara Brown Taylor, *Leaving Church: A Memoir of Faith* (San Francisco: HarperOne, 2012), 22–23.

Chapter Thirty-Two

Facing Down Mortality

I did not make it to the memorial service for Elvis today. I should have been there to honor the life of a very fine man, but I doubt I was missed at what was surely a well-attended event. I had a few reasons for not going, although I think the main one was that I didn't want to run into my friend Jeff and hear him say one more time, "We need to stop meeting like this."

The sad truth is I have grown weary of attending memorial services. The pace has picked up lately, with five other friends answering their last call in the past year. I look around, and all I see are widows.

I would like to chalk up this mortality trend to some random set of factors, but the truth is inescapable: I am getting older. The clearest sign I am aging is not the chronic aching left knee, the few extra pounds I resolve to lose each year, the food stains that appear on the front of my shirt out of nowhere, or the fact that I have no idea what the host of *Saturday Night Live* did to merit the role. Losing more friends than you gain each year is the most obvious indication that you are getting closer to the finish line.

The math is as simple as it is sobering. I recently celebrated my seventieth birthday, which means I am much nearer to the end of my life than its beginning. According to the Social Security Life Expectancy Calculator, the average life expectancy for an American male born in 1953 is eighty-five. That means the best estimate is I have only fifteen more years, or 780 weekends, left. I better find something memorable to do this Saturday night!

It's not like I am afraid of dying. I've had a good life. I experienced and achieved more than I could ever have imagined given my humble beginnings. I learned to be a decent guitar player and found ways to share my music with children and adults alike. I was fortunate to spend most of my life in the good company of Sandy, my wife and abiding love. My two sons enjoy my company. I have a daughter-in-law whom I consider to be the daughter I never had. My two grandchildren delight me when they ask for "Pappy-back rides" as they leave our home. They take charge of our journey, directing me along a circuitous route to their car on the street. Their addition to our family made me wonder why we waited so long to become grandparents.

I am not afraid to face down my own mortality, to say goodbye to this wonderful life and the beautiful world around me. My friend and folk philosopher Hank summed it up this way one night when he said, "When you're dead, you don't know it. All the pain is felt by others. The same thing happens when you're stupid."

We all laughed and asked Hank to repeat it. At first, I latched on to the closing punch line, which reminded me of the lunacy that flows out of the mouths of far too many contemporary politicians. But then I thought about the widows of my friends who were still feeling the sting of their loss, and the joke didn't seem quite so funny. I imagined them forced to make hasty decisions on a myriad of matters to which they had given no prior thought. What were his favorite hymns? Bible verses? Who should speak at his service? And so on, and so on.

Questions like these, and countless others, are best answered without the strain and pain induced by the loss of a loved one. But that is seldom the case. According to a 2015 national survey conducted by the Harris Poll on behalf of the Funeral and Memorial Information Council, 60 percent of adults over the age of forty indicated they would prefer to prearrange their own service. However, only 17 percent had done so, suggesting a lot of widows, widowers, and children will face unnecessary funeral-planning pressure someday.

There are numerous websites that provide detailed checklists of decisions that must be made to honor the departed. While I am sure they are helpful, one contains more than ninety items to address, offering a staggering to-do list at a time when those left behind are overwhelmed with grief.

To spare my loved ones from the angst that comes with that kind of choice overload, I thought it would be helpful to share in advance wishes that could make my end-of-life celebration particular to me. Since no humans are the same, it follows that gatherings held to honor the life of a loved one should be a unique reflection of who they were. Here are some thoughts on how to make mine express what made me, me.

- **Guests**: Anyone and everyone should be invited and allowed to attend whatever event happens. We don't need to erect any more barriers on this earth. Beyond immediate family and friends, I hope all three members of the Holy Trinity will be there since each played a role in my life. I always felt God was *above* me, and I looked up to him or her for strength. I know Jesus walked *beside* me, guiding my way and offering the example for how we should treat others, especially "the least of these." I often felt the presence of the Holy Spirit *around* me, steering me away from trouble as I journeyed through this world.

  I am hoping all three will find a way to participate in the festivities. Our Heavenly Father might lead the Lord's Prayer (more on this later). Jesus could turn water into wine so we don't run out. As for the Holy Spirit, while we might not be able to see it, I suspect it will work the crowd in helpful and mysterious ways I cannot possibly define.

- **Dress Code**: No suits or ties. No formal dresses. No black attire. Only vivid, primary colors. Everyone should wear something in their favorite color from childhood. My choice will be cobalt blue. What's yours?

- **Scripture**: Standard practice suggests a passage should be read from both testaments of the Bible. My Old Testament selection was inspired by a handwritten thank-you note I received from my father a few years before his death endorsing Micah 6:8 as words to live by. The verse reads: "What does the Lord require of you but to do justice, and to love kindness, and to walk humbly with your God?" Solid advice from a very wise man.

  For the New Testament reading, I cannot go wrong choosing one of Mother Teresa's favorite texts, Mathew 25:40: "Truly I tell you, whatever you did for one of the least of these brothers and sisters of mine, you did for me."

  Both passages speak to matters of justice, mercy, caring, and humility—values I cared a great deal about but regret not doing more to address during my time here.

- **Eulogy**: A few years ago I became intrigued by comments made about the deceased at memorial services. I began to wonder what I could learn about a person I had never met from their eulogy. I developed an idea for a book project, a series of short stories about common folk whose lives were revealed through what was said about them on the day family and friends came together to bid them a final farewell. *Funeral Crasher* would be an insightful exploration into the qualities of life as represented in the stories told about the departed.

I went back and forth, debating the merits of the idea. Perhaps it would be insensitive for a stranger, a voyeur if you will, to appear at a time and place where loved ones were in mourning. In the end, I abandoned the idea not out of the sheer creepiness that had made it intriguing but after I heard eulogies that failed to capture my understanding of the deceased. "Did the pastor grab the wrong file as he rushed out of his office and headed to the pulpit?" I wondered.

The train of thought driving a eulogy can run off the rails in at least two distinct ways, both of which result in a portrayal that bears no resemblance to their subject. In some cases, the eulogist spins a yarn so outlandish that loved ones are unable to recognize the deceased. Maybe it stems from a desire to wish them into heaven, or a sense of guilt for failing to say how they felt about them when they were alive. I don't know.

A memorable scene from the novel *The Adventures of Tom Sawyer* demonstrates how far afield a eulogy can stray, when the pastor offers an exaggerated portrayal of Mark Twain's fictional hero. It is a Sunday afternoon after Tom, Huck Finn, and Bob vanished in a flood downriver. The townspeople who gathered for their funeral are treated to a tall tale all its own as the minister rewrites their histories. Here is an excerpt (with omissions for clarity):

As the service proceeded, the clergyman drew such pictures of the graces, the winning ways, and the rare promise of the lost lads that every soul there . . . felt a pang in remembering that he had . . . persistently seen only faults and flaws in the poor boys. The minister related many a touching incident in the lives of the departed, too, which illustrated their sweet, generous natures, and the people could easily see, now, how noble and beautiful those episodes were.[1]

The minister rewrote their life histories. Tom and his friends were no longer considered rapscallions. They were lost heroes (at least until they showed up in person a few minutes later).

An example of the other extreme comes from the memorial service for a former colleague of mine. Chris was a person I had come to depend on at work. Simple in appearance and tastes, wise beyond her years and pay grade, Chris could be counted on to offer the kind of perspective that corporate executives like me, who think they have all the answers, needed to hear. Chris possessed the gift of perspective bestowed on her through a life that involved more personal pain and hardship than is probably fair.

Following her death from an illness that took her from us too soon, Chris's sister and a close friend scrambled to pull together a memorial service at a modest funeral home instead of a church. Chris, you see, was not at all religious. While her sister was reaching out to me to speak, Chris's friend asked her own father to offer remarks as well. A retired Baptist minister struck me as an odd choice given Chris's agnostic stance, but I assumed the man knew Chris and trusted everything would work out fine.

I was wrong. The preacher commandeered the service to deliver a fire-and-brimstone message about the torments of hell scary enough to make even the strongest believer quake in their boots. For twenty minutes that seemed like an eternity, he ripped through our grief like an evangelical tsunami, warning an audience of complete strangers that the wages of sin were death, urging us to repent and accept the gospel message. At least there was no altar call to prolong matters.

I fumed at the insensitivity reflected in words that lacked any connection to Chris, making her life unrecognizable in the moment. He had made no effort to learn about her beliefs (or lack of them). Instead, in front of about fifty of her colleagues and a handful of family members, a "man of God" turned a memorial service into a revival and, in the process, sentenced my friend to eternal damnation. Maybe he saved some lost soul that day, but I doubt it.

After the preacher returned to his seat, I took the podium to share my reflections on Chris. I said, "For those of you who knew Chris well, I hope my comments reflect some of your own thoughts and feelings about her. And I hope you may find some comfort through recalling some of the things about Chris that you may not have noticed. For those here today who may not have known Chris well, I hope these comments provide some insight into why she remains so dear to our hearts today."

My prayer is that I painted an authentic picture of Chris that day and restored some dignity to the memory of this good, if not godly, woman in the process.

My colleague Chris and fictional Tom Sawyer hold one thing in common: their eulogies missed the mark. Memorial services are a time to hold that dear one up and share enough about the person to remind us why we will miss them. Eulogists cannot always be trusted, so no eulogies for me, thank you.

What shall be done instead? I suggest a storytelling exercise where family and friends pair off and share a memory or two of me with others. Maybe it is about something good I did, a funny anecdote, a silly blunder, or a way I helped. Everything is fair game. In that way, my life can be remembered through the eyes of many who knew me, not just a single set with impaired vision.

- **Prayer**: Have you ever encountered that awkward moment when you are not certain which words to use when speaking the Lord's Prayer? Since most of us believe there is only one God, having multiple versions of the universal prayer seems like a liturgical oxymoron to me. As I understand it, Wycliffe, who lived in the fourteenth century, used the word *debts* in his translation, while Tyndale chose the word *trespasses* in his sixteenth-century version. This strikes me as a difference without distinction, a trivial vestige from the past.

    My view: neither version is preferred because the operative word here is *forgive*, right? My desire is that both versions be spoken on that day, one after the other. The order will be determined by a coin toss like you see before an NFL game. A representative from the Catholic and Protestant teams will participate in a ceremonial coin flip (perhaps administered by the Holy Spirit) where the winner will choose which version will be spoken first. My hope is that regardless of which sideline you are on, this unifying prayer will be spoken twice with equal enthusiasm.

- **Music**: Music has been a big part of my life. I covered a lot of sonic terrain over the years, so we should do the same on this special occasion. We will work off a playlist that captures key aspects of my life. They are songs I loved, ones that spoke to me at different stages of my life.

On Childhood: "In My Room," by the Beach Boys

On Sports: "Centerfield," by John Fogerty

On Love (for Sandy): "Time in a Bottle," by Jim Croce

On Work: "Peace of Mind," by Boston

On Faith: "Running on Faith" by Eric Clapton

On Others: "Kindness," by Ryan Adams

On Self: "Simple Man," by Graham Nash

On Mortality: "Keep Me in Your Heart," by Warren Zevon

There are no hymns on my list. I can think of many I would love everyone to sing, but one thing I know for certain: "For All the Saints" will not be one of them. I have heard this hymn at many recent memorial services, and it frightens the bejesus out of me. One reason behind this visceral reaction is I am certain it was chosen because the deceased failed to make their musical preferences known, leaving their loved ones at the mercy of a church music director who defaults to this hymn. While it may work as a hymn of hope at an All Saints' Day service, the song (particularly the fourth verse) overwhelms me with despair through an onslaught of military references: fortress, captain, well-fought fight, strife, warfare, arms. I hold too much hope for lasting peace on earth to give that song any more airtime.

- **Farewell Reception**: Tom Sawyer stumbled into an interesting concept—being present at one's own funeral. I realize he did not expect to attend the event, but I think it is an idea worth exploring. Perhaps we should hold a one-stop reception and memorial service before the person passes away so they can be there too. We could call it a *living wake*, or maybe a *pre-morial service*. Regardless of what we call it, it would be an occasion where family and friends meet to say goodbye.

This was exactly what my mother's lifelong friend did as her final days approached. After the doctors delivered Marion the sentence of terminal cancer, she declared her wish for quality of life until its end. Marion took control of the narrative of her final days, holding an open-house celebration of her life the month before she died. Dozens of friends and family came to reminisce and say their farewells. How perfect!

I know God has final say on whether something like this will be possible in my case, but I can't help but envision it. I see my "pre-morial" event happening late in the afternoon under the shade of the live oak trees that define the perimeter of our backyard. People can come and go as they please, grab an adult beverage, and eat as many slices of my favorite food (pizza) as they like. At the appointed time, we will pause to hear scripture, say the Lord's Prayer twice, and listen to music selections that made up the soundtrack of my life.

- **Closing Scene**: As the sun sinks toward the horizon, we will all raise our glasses high in the air and sing a benediction toast to "The Parting Glass." This traditional Scottish song traces back to the early seventeenth century, its name derived from the final hospitality offered to a departing guest.[2] This custom has been practiced in several continents for centuries and remains very popular in Ireland, where the song is often sung at the end of a gathering of friends. After one of my musician friends blows the pitch pipe providing the opening note, we will begin to sing:

Of all the money that e'er I had,

I spent it in good company.

And all the harm that e'er I did,

alas, it was to none but me.

And all I've done for want of wit,

to memory now I can't recall.

So fill to me the parting glass;

good night and joy be to you all.

So fill to me the parting glass,

and gather as the evening falls.

And gently rise and softly call,

"Good night and joy be to you all."

I have pondered the meaning of this song since I first heard it more than a decade ago. Is it about one gentleman's polite exit from a neighborhood pub before closing time? Or is this a metaphor about leaving this earthly life to head for another that awaits? I like each interpretation so much I hold them together in my mind, accepting them as two sides of the same precious coin.

As daylight dims, I will say my final farewells, eternally grateful for being gifted with one last chance to say "Thank you" for the unconditional love bestowed on me by so many. They are what made my life matter.

- **Next Stop**: I loved this life. I look forward to the next one where I can personally thank those already there who taught me so much here:

To Dr. Hamming, for giving more than a lesson in geography.

To Bob, who showed me that caring for others reveals the best in ourselves.

To my colleague, Chris, who forced me to not take myself so seriously.

To my musician friend, John, who left us all something to remember him by.

To all the children, who pointed me toward regaining a sense of wonder.

To my dear father, who showed me how to live the legacy that is my life every day.

And to many, many more.

As for the rest of you, keep living out your life to its fullest. Tell those you love how you feel. Then tell them again. And when your final day arrives, know that I will be waiting there to greet you in an afterworld our mortal minds can only imagine—a place where the sun always shines, the wine bottles are always full, there are no guns, everyone can sing on key, and no one ever has to say goodbye.

Buen Camino!

---

[1] Mark Twain, *The Adventures of Tom Sawyer* (Hartford: American Publishing Company, 1876), 268.

[2] Wikipedia, s.v. "Folk music," last modified January 13, 2023, 15:58, https://en.wikipedia.org/wiki/Folk_music.

Summary of Part IV: Transcendent Power

Lessons I Have Learned from my Relationship with God

➢ Scatter seeds through good deeds. Greater forces will protect and nurture your kindly act and make it grow into something beyond your wildest dreams.

➢ Leave something to remember. We all hope to be remembered after we are gone. What will you leave behind to make that wish come true?

➢ Believe in providence. Recognize that unexpected outcomes may be due to God's benevolent and timely intervention rather than fate, chance, or coincidence.

➢ Live your legacy. Use your life to reveal a system of belief and behavior that endures long after you are gone.

➢ Believe in things not seen. In your service to others, have faith that something positive came from your effort even if you may not see it with your own eyes.

➢ Find thin places. Take a journey into God's creation, and open your heart to be touched by "something bigger."

➢ Believe and behold. In order to bring meaning and understanding to your life, consider how the *lessons* you've learned from others and the *experiences* you've personally had inform and illuminate each other.

➢ Plan your finale. Share with those close to you how you want your farewell celebration to be a unique reflection of who you are.

Part V: Integration and Intentionality

I organized the stories in this book around four separate themes: (1) my understanding of myself, (2) my relationships with others, (3) my appreciation for the world around me, and (4) my connection with the transcendent power of God. This final section provides a summary of what experience has taught me about these four distinct relationships and how they converge to define who I am. It also offers ways to be intentional in fostering an ongoing personal connection to these different dimensions of life.

Chapter Thirty-Three

The One and Only Me

What is a life? The older I get, the more I wonder and the clearer it becomes that I may never know. My current answer is that a life is composed of personal moments that, in their everyday profundity, offer meaning and reveal that we each are a precious part of something bigger. Whether our time here was granted with fame, failure, or something in between, it is through our stories that we come to understand two contradictory truths: (1) each of us is unique, and (2) we all have much in common.

Here is my summary of our four relationships and how they point to what I call "the one and only me."

My Relationship with Myself—"Be Engaged"

I began with stories of milestone experiences that provided insight into how I can become a better version of myself. I learned that we each possess strengths and talents that make us uniquely who we are. Left untended, however, these assets can grow into liabilities. The path forward requires a commitment to excellence, which is easier once you identify personal passions that demand your attention and contribute to a richer and fuller life.

While there is little in life we fully control, one of the more powerful levers we can push or pull in the face of challenges is the mindset we choose to adopt. Our mindset *is* ours to manage, and a good place to start exercising this capability is by letting go of slights from the past. In a virtuous cycle of sorts, positive behaviors contribute to more positive attitudes. Managing your mindset becomes the key ingredient in taking care of yourself so you can be there physically and emotionally for others when they need you.

To be in relationship with oneself, one must "be engaged" in life to keep learning and adjusting every day to become a better version of "the one and only you."

My Relationships with Others—"Bestow"

While I did not write about them here, the stories in this section reminded me of countless individuals whose caring support gifted me with new ways of seeing myself. They were people like the following:

- The high school coach who kicked this three-year four-letter senior off the track team to teach me much-needed lessons. Coach Mike showed me the importance of setting priorities, making difficult choices, and communicating decisions clearly to those who need to know.

- The colleague at my first job who brought me under his wing as a mentor and offered me the priceless gift of perspective. Sam was so good at this role that I didn't realize that I had been his protégé until years later.

- Mary Jane, the elderly woman from my church who encouraged me to share my musical talents with others. She coaxed confidence into the shy musician hiding inside me. She was the catalyst in my evolution from playing guitar and singing privately (an audience of one) to offering my music as a service to others.

What they had in common was that they saw something worth celebrating or correcting in me that I did not see in myself. Each offered me their wisdom, expecting nothing in return. They imparted gifts upon me in ways I can never fully repay, except by doing the same for others.

Since none of us navigate through this life alone, we must be open to asking others for their help. Because relationships don't just happen, we must be willing to make the first move that opens up lanes of understanding on how we can best serve each other. How we treat others is a reflection of ourself, making it a duty to go out and "bestow" our welcoming presence, our gift of caring and kindness to the next person we see. Let empathy be your guide as you affirm the value of the other, even if that requires stretching the truth a bit. The great thing about this is that when you give of yourself by being there for others, you gain as much or more in return.

My Relationship with the World Around Me—"Be Here"

The third section dealt with relationships with the worlds through which we navigate. I defined a *world* to be anywhere we live and grow, hurt and heal. These may be big or small, public or private spaces where life gets reframed and refreshed once we make a conscious effort to engage in it.

Shaking up daily routines can serve as a catalyst because it forces us to "be here," to slow down and pay attention instead of sleepwalking through each day. Pushing ourselves to explore unfamiliar worlds has a way of making us stronger. By embracing a beginner's mind, we can engage the familiar in new and wonderful ways and, more importantly, find inspiration as a result.

But beware: you might notice problems and inequities that trouble you, things that just don't seem the way they should. Avoid the temptation to sit back and complain, because that is only a waste of your energy and everyone else's time. Instead, define what needs to be done, whether that be something big or little but definitely important. Look for ways to help others convince themselves to join the cause. Define what success looks like, because the result you demand of yourself and others is the result you are likely to get.

My Relationship with God—"Behold"

The fourth section considered my relationship with the transcendent—or, in the religious tradition in which I was raised, simply God. As we roam this earth, I wonder if we are human beings in search of spiritual experiences or spiritual beings living human ones. I don't know. But I do know that the universe speaks to us through our experiences, so seek out those places where you can connect with God and feel his or her presence in your life. Scatter seeds of good will, having the faith that a greater power will make something positive come from that even if you never see it with your own eyes. Find inspiration from those who showed you how to live a good life or left you something to remember them by. Be on the lookout for moments when you can "behold" a holy presence that challenges and enriches what you have been taught to believe so that you can make it your own.

Integration—"Becoming"

We are human beings, belonging to the species known as *homo sapiens*. It is an umbrella label that portrays a static and undifferentiated view of your life and mine. Nothing could be less true because each of us is a unique and unfinished individual. More than just human beings, we are "humans becoming"—changing and growing through all that life has to offer. It is our responsibility to ensure the entire range of life experiences inform and guide us through an ongoing process of discovering (and rediscovering) "the one and only me."

This concept of integration is visually depicted in the following illustration.

(FIGURE B HERE)

***

Intentionality

Writing stories about these four types of relationships awakened me to the fact that I am in constant connection with each, whether I realize it or not. Living out one's life provides an opportunity to stop, notice, and reflect on what one has seen and felt and become. This led me to wonder how I could be more intentional in connecting with each element of the relational-consciousness framework every day. To that end, I have been following two practices that heighten an ongoing awareness and sensitivity to the four dimensions and foster reflection about recent experiences.

- **Living in the Present**: Since life consists of a series of singular moments, we must find ways to live out each one to the fullest. My way to kindle my connection with the four types of relationships in the here and now is through an affirmation comprised of five statements, one for each of the four types of relationships and a fifth that reminds me to integrate all of this into who I am becoming.[1] It goes like this:

  "There is nothing I would rather be doing." (Self)

  "There is no one I would rather be with." (Others)

  "There is no place I would rather be." (World)

  "I will look for a Divine presence here." (God)

  "This will become a part of the one and only me." (Integration)

  These simple lines force me to pause and take stock of what I am doing, thinking, feeling, and sensing. They help me recognize and capture the fullness of life in real time. They leave me knowing I am different now than I was only a few moments earlier.

- **Pausing to Reflect**: This practice requires taking a few minutes each month (or whatever time frame works for you) to reflect on recent experiences that offered insight into each type of relationship. Here is a list of questions designed to facilitate that process:

In the past month . . .

- "What new things have I learned about myself and life?" (Self)

- "How have I connected with and helped people I have been with?" (Others)

- "What have I discovered from all that surrounds me?" (World)

- "Where have I felt a Divine presence?" (God)

- "How am I becoming a better version of the one and only me?" (Integration)

Writing down my answers to these questions provides me a new starting point from which I can continue to grow going forward, one month at a time.

---

[1] In his book *The Way is Made by Walking* (pp. 134–137), author Arthur Paul Boers described walking the Camino de Santiago as a "focal experience." Boers cited social philosopher Albert Borgmann as the source of an affirmation like the one I share here. According to Boers, Borgmann would ask his students to identify the last time they were able to affirm the following:

"There is no place I would rather be.
There is nothing I would rather do.
There is no one I would rather be with.
This I will remember well."

Chapter Thirty-Four

Redemption from Pluto

In 1991, civic leader John W. Gardner delivered the commencement address at Stanford, one hundred years after the university was founded. The speech imparted wisdom such as this for the audience of graduates:

> *The lessons of maturity aren't simple things such as acquiring information and skills. You learn not to engage in self-destructive behavior, not to burn up energy in anxiety. You learn to manage your tensions. . . . You find that self-pity and resentment are among the most toxic of drugs. You conclude that the world loves talent but pays off on character.*[1]

Today, I am embarrassed by the "toxicity" of self-pity that ran through my veins during my time in the company of Pluto. I wasted energy that I can never recoup, lost time I can never regain. Part of the problem, to be sure, was that I had become so tied up in career and success that I failed to adequately value the other slices of my life. Nor did I realize how much I still had to offer, even as my star (or planet) was in its decline. I cannot go back and fix any of that now. My hope is that through this book project, I have found some degree of redemption.

Will Pluto ever regain full membership as the most distant planet in our solar system? From what I read, it seems doubtful. Some scientists continue to argue that Pluto was unfairly removed from its lofty status in 2006. The International Astronomical Union, which has the power to assign official names and statuses of celestial bodies, does not appear inclined to reverse their pronouncement that Pluto failed to exert enough power and influence to deserve the prestigious title.

My connection with that lonely ex-planet was mere happenstance, the coincidental timing of our mutual decline. While Pluto must depend on others for its redemption, I came to realize I could do that for myself. That is why I wrote this book—to atone for my failure to seize the wisdom-sharing opportunity available in my final corporate role.

I am painfully aware that I have not lived out all the advice I have offered through these stories. Writing down one's beliefs does not make them reality, but it does offer a valuable starting point. I do know that the process of writing these stories allowed me to consider the people and events that have developed my understanding of myself and the universe that surrounds me. It awakened me to ways I can be a better me today and tomorrow. My deepest hope is that these stories have helped you do the same.

Let it be so. Peace to you all!

---

[1] "John W. Gardner's Address at Stanford's 100th Commencement Ceremony," John W. Gardner Center for Youth and their Communities, Stanford University, June 16, 2016, https://gardnercenter.stanford.edu/news/john-w-gardners-address-stanfords-100th-commencement-ceremony.

Appendix

25 Things I Have Learned from 25 Years in the Business

Presentation to Pizza Hut Marketing Department
February 5, 2008

1. If Something Is Not Working or Is Annoying, Fix It!
    a. Applies to Conference-Room Tables, Data Reports, and Consumer Problems
2. *You* Control Your Own Mood and Mindset
    a. Viktor Frankl Quotation from *Man's Search for Meaning*
3. Avoid Raising Issues or Problems without Suggesting a Solution
4. When Considering a Job Change, Have a Compelling Reason to Go (Not Just Reasons to Leave)
    a. Appreciate What You Have
    b. The Grass Is *Not Always* Greener
5. In Business, Everyone Can Be Replaced (Including You)
    a. Companies Have Short-Term Memories
    b. You Will Be Forgotten
    c. What is Past Matters Very Little
    d. Lyrics from "Glory Days," by Bruce Springsteen
6. Leveraging Your Personal Strengths Is More Important than Trying to Improve Your Weaknesses
    a. Just Don't Allow the Latter to Become Glaring Ones
7. Lacking Information from You, Others Will Fill in the Gaps (and Not Necessarily with the Most Positive Angle)
    a. Communicate, Communicate, Communicate
    b. Especially Relevant for Introverts
8. The Most Important Job in Marketing is Correctly Defining the Category in Which You Want to Compete
    a. Frames of Reference
    b. Competitive Set
    c. Sources of Growth
9. Hang Out with Kids
    a. They Are Real, Genuine, and True
    b. They Have No Hidden Agendas
    c. If You're a Parent, Don't Let Raising Them Get in the Way of Knowing Them as People
    d. If You're Not a Parent, Borrow Somebody Else's

e. Or Go Read a Book to the Little Ones at the Children's Center
10. Clear Thinking and Direction Trumps More Data Every Time
    a. Patrick Lencioni quotation from *The Five Temptations of a CEO*
11. Address Performance Issues Honestly and in a Timely Manner
12. Trust Your Intuition (It's Probably Right!)
    a. Malcolm Gladwell quotation from *Blink*
13. Don't Place the Onus for Creativity on the Consumer
    a. It's Our Job to Anticipate Their Needs and to Create Solutions
14. Measurements, and the Incentives That Go with Them, Can Bring about Unintended Consequences
    a. What We Measure Matters a Lot
    b. You Get What You Measure (and More)
15. Everything Is Discoverable
    a. MySpace and Facebook are Replacing Private Investigators
    b. Be Careful What You Type
16. You Are Likely to Learn More Spending an Hour with a Consumer on Their Turf than from Most Research Reports
    a. Get Out of Your Office and into the World
    b. In Return, You Will Gain Empathy and Find Conviction
17. Take Moments to Stop, Look, Listen, and See Beauty
    a. Don't Allow the Pursuit of Your Goals Make You Miss Out on the Journey
18. Work Happier!
    a. Pizza Is a Fun Category (Are We Taking It Too Seriously?)
    b. Let Its Lightness Inspire our Imaginations
19. Learn to Let Go of Past Slights
    a. Grudges Create Immense Negative Energy
20. What You Believe Will Give You Happiness in Your Career May Change over Time
    a. Stay Flexible and Open
    b. Reexamine and Reassess
21. Practice Level Blindness
    a. "Build strong, positive relationships with the bottom 40% of students. They become the parents you have to deal with later (as school board members)."
        —My Brother-in-Law Don Logan, Benton (IA) Community HS
22. Learn to Adapt Your Style for Different Situations, Bosses, and Teams
    a. You Own Making the Relationships Work
23. Find a Passion Outside of Work
    a. It Helps You Recognize it in Others
    b. It Helps You Stay in Balance
24. Good Startings and Endings Are What Matter Most

a. "Aoccdrnig to a rscheearch at Cmabrigde Uinervisty, it deosn't mttaer in waht oredr the ltteers in a wrod are. The olny iprmoetnt tihng is taht the frist and lsat ltteer be at the rghit pclae. The rset can be a tatol mses and you can sitll raed it wouthit porbelm. This is bcuseae the huamn mnid deos not raed ervey lteter by istlef, but the wrod as a wlohe. Amzanig, huh?"

25. Never Stop Learning
    a. "When you think you are coasting, you are going downhill." —Frank Sinatra

About the Author

Larry Dykstra, author of *Music on a Mission* and *In the Service of My Country*, discovered that as his business career ended, he had much more to learn.

In 2010, Larry began a journey to broaden his focus and rebalance his life's priorities. Curious by nature and a lifelong intentional learner, he pursued experiences that introduced him to new worlds and stretched him as a person, including playing music with and for others, serving hospitalized children, and exploring matters of spirituality and healing.

Over the next six years, Larry spent more than six hundred hours in children's hospitals as a therapeutic music entertainer and as a chaplain in the Pastoral Care Department. In the process, he discovered that he could no longer define success by what he did for a living but by what he did for others.

A self-taught musician, Larry is gifted in leading informal sing-alongs that engage audiences. He is a member of multiple ensembles playing genres ranging from R&B to acoustic rock to worship. Depending on the group, song, and audience, Larry handles a combination of rhythm guitar, mandolin, and lead or backup vocals.

As a speaker at professional research and marketing events, Larry has produced original viewpoints on topics such as the consumer-insight discipline, innovation, group decision-making, and communication. Larry remains connected to the business world by providing strategic planning, consumer insight, and product-innovation services for numerous well-known companies as a consultant partner for Flight3 Marketing.

Larry currently resides in Dallas, Texas, and has been married to his best friend, Sandy, for forty-two years. "Taco Tuesday" family dinners with Sandy; their sons, Charlie and Evan;

Charlie's wife, Molly; and their two grandchildren, Emerson and Owen, are his favorite part of

each week.

Book Summary

Life's connections are what grow us, shape us, and transform us as we learn to navigate each relationship—our relationships with ourselves, with others, with the world around us, and with God. But how can you be sure you're approaching each connection with the care and intentionality needed for a rich and fulfilling life?

Larry Dykstra brings decades' worth of stories and perceptive commentary to the table in *My Redemption from Pluto*, sharing the lessons he's realized along the way. He prompts every reader to be mindful of their mindsets, listen to learn, and rediscover wonder, among many other sincere encouragements. As you read his personal anecdotes and thought-provoking insights, pause to consider how each might apply to your own life story—and you might be surprised by how much wisdom can be gleaned just by slowing down and reflecting on each connection you have.

www.ingramcontent.com/pod-product-compliance
Lightning Source LLC
Chambersburg PA
CBHW022047050726
47591CB00002B/424